THE
John Foster Dulles
BOOK OF
HUMOR

Louis Jefferson (right) with Eisenhower's Secretary of State, John Foster Dulles

THE
John Foster Dulles
BOOK OF
HUMOR

BY

Louis Jefferson

St. Martin's Press
New York

Library of Congress Cataloging-in-Publication Data

Jefferson, Louis.
  The John Foster Dulles book of humor.

    1. Dulles, John Foster, 1889-1959—Anecdotes.
2. Jefferson, Louis. 3. Statesmen—United States—
Anecdotes, facetiae, satire, etc. I. Title.
E748.D868J44   1986   973.921′092′4 [B]   86-1972
ISBN 0-312-44355-2

First Edition

10 9 8 7 6 5 4 3 2 1

To Jennifer and Douglas
Who Were Always in My Heart

"Lou, you are a very improbable security officer."
—John Foster Dulles

"Lou, you saw things that none of the rest of us saw."
—Janet Avery Dulles

Contents

PREFACE

History has put a cold face on John Foster Dulles. The image we are given is, more often than not, inhuman. Yet Foster Dulles was, if nothing else, a very human man. I was his personal security officer (bodyguard) for nearly five years, and we became close. Shortly after his death, his widow, and my friend, Janet Avery Dulles, said to me, "Lou, you knew him better than most, how he really was—you saw the humor in things—and I know you kept notes. I hope you write some of it one day, if only for the grandchildren. . . ."

If some of what follows seems imprecise, that is because the world I write about is precise only in fiction, or in fact that is based on fiction. And if, at times, it seems that something is left out, it undoubtedly is. The years have made certain events possible to put on paper. For others, there have not been enough years. So, loose ends will appear in ways that a good novelist would never allow. But this is not a spy drama. Nor is it comedy, or soap opera, although it has elements of them all, because that's the way it was.

THE
John Foster Dulles
BOOK OF
HUMOR

1

Political Science

Dwight David Eisenhower, President of the United
States, glanced across the White House lawn at the
retreating back of his Vice-President, Richard Nixon,
squinted at his Secretary of State, John Foster Dulles, and
growled, "Foster, the trouble with Dick Nixon is he never
screwed enough women!"

When I heard this news, I decided on the spot to retire
my favorite presidential campaign button—IKE & DICK—
SURE TO CLICK.

As for Dulles, he just snorted surprise, and his face became one large twitch. The "Secretary for Earth and Air,"
as one commentator had described him, appeared, for a
moment, to be sliding his chin right down below his collar line. When this effort failed, he snorted again and responded, "Well, Mr. President, that is certainly an . . .
unusual . . . view."

In the intervening years, I have heard hundreds of theories on "the trouble with Dick Nixon"—most of them fallacious—but none so succinct as Eisenhower's. The general-turned-President really seemed to relish the thought, and his voice had resonance as he bored in on Dulles with, "You agree, huh?"

Dulles had his face in place again, but it was difficult to determine if he was covering a laugh with a shudder, or a shudder with a laugh, as he gasped a reply to his chief. "Well," he gurgled through the down side of his mouth, "Mr. President, there *is* his wife, Pat."

"Where?" Eisenhower barked, whirling his head about while, at the same time, putting on his professor-trying-to-look-like-a-general look, knowing full well that the "look" came out the other way around. It confused people, and he knew it. A valuable tactic.

"Well, now," Dulles replied, sounding confused, "Pat's always stood with Dick . . ."

"*Near* him," Eisenhower corrected.

"Near him?" Dulles questioned.

"Yes, Foster. *Near* him," Eisenhower said coldly. "There's a difference."

"*Near* him as opposed to *with* . . . ?" Dulles asked, puzzled, his lawyer's passion for distinctions aroused.

"Yes," Eisenhower hissed.

"You mean . . . ?" Dulles murmured.

"Yes," Eisenhower hissed again.

"Well," the Secretary crunched, "Dick does have some, uh, capabilities in foreign affairs."

"Foreign *policy*, Foster, policy," Eisenhower said, dryly.

"I see," Dulles said, clearing his throat vigorously, and adding, as an afterthought, "The Vice-President *did* come to see me in the basement the other day."

"In the basement!" Eisenhower exploded. "*The State Department basement?*"

"He didn't want to be seen," Dulles said softly. "I told

him that it would be easier if he just came in the front door, but he said that he wasn't looking for the 'easy way.'"

"I'll bet," Eisenhower muttered, adding, "One thing about Dick—he does not view life as the pursuit of comfort."

"The Vice-President has been loyal to you," Dulles said. "He has his good points."

"Of course he does!" Eisenhower said. "It's just that he can't seem to get some of his damned insecurities off his sleeve. I mean, to think of it—the *State Department basement!*"

Actually, the then Vice-President Nixon had summoned Dulles to the Sate Department's basement for "briefings" on more than one occasion. His need for secrecy in this regard was never adequately explained, although I knew that he suffered from what I call "wagon-train morality," i.e., do what's right, but, above all, protect yourself. He was probably influenced by his belief that the State Department bureaucracy hated him—a not altogether inaccurate judgment. But, it was more than that. He was *always* cautious, careful. It was as if he had spent most of his life in solitary confinement. His personality, even back then, seemed automatically to dictate secrecy. In this instance, the secret itself was a secret. We kept secret from people normally in the basement, such as drivers, messengers, and guards, the fact that they were witnessing a secret when they saw Nixon, because if they had known that it was a secret, we believed that they might have talked about it. By treating Nixon's visits as routine, hardly anyone even noticed. Eventually Nixon asked me about what he termed the "tightness" of the security around "my meetings with the Secretary." He tried to force his eyes right into mine as he added, "No one must know. *No* one. It will be misunderstood."

As best I could, I explained our not-secret-because-it-is-secret-in-order-to-keep-it-secret approach. Nixon listened, nodded sagely, and gave me what I used to call his "circular stare," because it came right at you even though it was going round and round. It made me nervous. I asked, "What do you think, Mr. Vice-President?"

He just kept nodding sagely. His eyes were watering when he finally said, "The only thing is, uh, if we tell them—those people who work down there—that it's a secret, and, uh, then they *know* they are seeing a secret, and, well, I mean, let's just say, that is, that if they *do* know it's secret, and, then, they *tell* somebody *because* it is a secret, and then, you see, if we *catch* them, then, uh, ahhh then, we, uh, *have* them, and, well, when we've actually *caught* them at it, well, then, you see . . . ahhhhh."

I thought he was having an orgasm, but I just smiled my admiration of his "wisdom" as I wondered at its strangeness.

Nixon often gave me the feeling that he was one of those people who never stop searching for the room where the secret of life is kept in a box, even while knowing that it does not exist. His eyes were always scanning, seeking, asking, but never answering. Although it is not fashionable to say so, I kind of liked him. He reminded me of a piece of precious china, with a crack in it.

On one elevator ride back up from a meeting with the Vice-President, Dulles burst out, "I told Dick Nixon that we saw Jack Kennedy coming out of the bushes in Georgetown with his fly open."

I showed my surprise. My mouth dropped down toward my belt buckle. A few nights earlier we *had* seen Senator John F. Kennedy dart out from behind bushes by a house that was not his and run down a quiet Georgetown street. He was in shirtsleeves, and appeared to be struggling to hold up his pants. Pulling my mouth back up from my belt buckle, I burped out some words. "You told *Nixon!*"

Dulles, unconcerned, said, "Yes. Did you find out who lives there?"

"Behind the bushes?"

"Of course," he grunted impatiently.

"Yes, sir, I did. Three young women."

"Terrible. Terrible. What about his wife—what's her name?"

"Jacqueline."

"Oh, yes. I think I met her. Attractive woman. Do you think she knows?"

"Well, Wiley Buchanan [Chief of Protocol] says if she's not used to it now, she'd better get used to it."

Dulles got a little leer into his eyes as he said, "Wiley would know, but Lyndon Johnson told me that Joe Kennedy was worse than any of his boys."

"Worse?" I asked.

"Worse." Dulles clucked.

"Worse?" I repeated.

"Women." Dulles grunted.

"Oh," I said, having seen the light a little slowly. "Well, Senator Johnson has himself been known to . . . er, uh . . ."

"Lyndon? Women?" Dulles asked, interest lighting up his face.

"Yes, sir."

"Where?"

"Well, for one—in the office."

"His office?" Dulles croaked.

"Right."

"You mean . . ."

"Yes."

"Good Lord!" he said, with genuine distress in his voice.

"Why, I was in his office just the other day, and, in fact
. . . he kept me waiting."

I didn't know what to say.

Dulles said, "Do you think, uh . . ."

"It is highly possible," I replied. "I was with you, and,
yes, that is probably what he was doing."

"Good heavens."

"Yes, well, you know, the receptionist . . ."

"She wasn't—Good Lord—there."

"Yes."

Dulles' eyes bugged right out through his thick glasses.
"You really think . . . the receptionist?"

"That's the rumor," I said, feeling myself on tricky
ground. "It's also said that there's a . . . rotation."

"I can't believe it."

"That's what I hear."

"Good Lord. Yes. Well. As for the Kennedys, well, Lyndon just doesn't like them—any of them."

"I know," I agreed. "His stories about them are generally scatological."

Dulles whooped. "*Scatological?*"

"Yes, sir. The American people may not be ready for the
Kennedys, or Lyndon Johnson, but are they ready for
scatology?"

Dulles gave a small laugh, and said, seriously, "Joe Kennedy wants Jack Kennedy to be president, but, you have a
point in an odd sort of way, and, besides, well . . ."

". . . all those women," I added for him.

"Hmmmmmmmmmm" came out between Dulles' teeth.

"I doubt if his women will hurt Kennedy politically," I
said. "The press probably won't write about it. If it was
Dick Nixon, they might, though, because, well, Dick
Nixon is . . . Dick Nixon."

Dulles nodded agreement, saying, "They sure don't
seem to have any trouble finding things to write about

Nixon. Sometimes I think they accuse him of practices he hasn't even heard of—but, you're right, I think, about women, that is, I don't think that there's anything to write about there, although he does have some unusual friends."

"I know," I said, not sure that I did, and wondering what Dulles meant by "practices."

Dulles made a face. "Joe McCarthy—awful man—says that Dick is afraid of J. Edgar Hoover. I find that hard to believe, but, there it is."

"Sir?"

"Something about Dick not wanting anyone to know certain things that Hoover knew. You know, people think that Dick and McCarthy and Hoover all operate together, are after the same thing, and so forth. So, they judge them together and that's a mistake."

"But McCarthy thinks Hoover has something on Nixon?"

"McCarthy says 'Hoover knows it all'—whatever that means. Anyway, whatever it is, according to Senator McCarthy, it scares Dick. You should know more about this than I do, shouldn't you?"

"I'm just the cop on your beat," I said lightly.

Dulles pinched his nose as if shutting out a strange smell. "I've never been called a 'beat' before."

"Only in a manner of speaking, Mr. Secretary, only in a manner of speaking." I paused and then added, "I heard one senator say that Joe McCarthy's main problem is that he wears his shirt collars too tight, and that slows the flow of oxygen to his brain. Me, I just think the guy drinks too much."

Dulles smiled, but his look was questioning. "I thought McCarthy was close to all you security people."

"I work for *you*, sir—the State Department."

"My brother Allen—others—say that McCarthy, the Senate, have infiltrated my security people."

"Well, Mr. Secretary," I said, "if McCarthy has 'infiltrated' the State Department, I'll bet that he's infiltrated your brother's CIA, too."

Dulles laughed. "I never thought of it that way. I'll tell Allen you said that . . . unless you'd rather I didn't."

"I don't want to get the CIA mad at me," I said, wondering what the CIA would do if it did get mad at me.

"Neither do I," Dulles murmured thoughtfully.

"Everybody talks about what McCarthy thinks about the State Department, but he also thinks the CIA's full of what he calls 'Ivy League Pinks.'"

"Extraordinary."

"Lyndon Johnson talks about Ivy League Pinks, too. In fact, Pink is complimentary, compared to some of the terms he uses about the Ivy League."

"I've heard him. But, whatever McCarthy thinks of the CIA, I'm sure that he has people here in the State Department."

"McCarthy says the *Soviets* have people here . . ."

We had left the elevator, and he was pacing the floor of his small, hideaway office when he said, disbelief etching every word, "Do you know that there are people who would rather have Soviet agents in the State Department than McCarthy or Senate agents?"

"Sounds funny," I said. "'Senate agents.'"

"I don't know that it is funny."

"Well, let's hope that all we have here at State is American agents."

"There are so many *kinds* of 'agents' these days," he said with weary resignation.

"It's a growth industry."

"Ha! I like that. Yes. But, as to Hoover, Nixon . . ."

"Vice-President Nixon *has* been involved in some serious affairs."

"Affairs?" Dulles barked.

"I was thinking of something like the Hiss 'affair.'"

"*Alger Hiss,*" Dulles crunched, adding, almost as an afterthought, "I never heard Nixon's relationship to Hiss described as an affair."

"No, sir, although it did tie them together forever in the
history books."

"Interesting way to look at it. I had a little problem over
Hiss. Talked into recommending him for a job. Do you
think he really was, or is, a Soviet agent?"

"I think it's quite possible."

"Of course, Hoover probably helped Nixon with the
Hiss matter—no question about it—and now Hoover
won't let him forget it, I suppose, or . . . something like
that," Dulles said, raking his fingers through thinning
hairs.

"That is certainly possible," I said.

"Did you know that General MacArthur had a problem
with women?"

Surprised at what seemed to be a change of subject, I
said, "No, sir."

"Before your time. The twenties. Thirties."

"His first wife?"

"Wife, indeed! Most people thought he had *one* mistress.
My information is that he had *three!*"

"At one time?"

"Possibly. Allen is the real expert on these matters, although I do remember quite a few stories myself. Mac-
Arthur wasn't all that unusual, you know. But lots of
things never get as far as the history books. That doesn't
mean these things don't happen. There was a French diplomat once who just wouldn't let my wife, Janet, alone.

Made me mad. He seemed to think it was his right or something. Arrogant fellow. Janet found it amusing, but I didn't. No, indeed. Never told anybody, but I did seriously consider getting out that pistol the Costa Rican gave me in 1915, and, well . . . but, I guess the age of duels has been over for quite a time."

I couldn't believe my ears. "What happened?" I asked.

"I finally told a friend—Jean Monnet—about it, and the fellow somehow disappeared.

"Sounds like the Mafia."

"No, no. Nothing like that. These things *can* be handled, you know."

"I see," I responded. Actually, I didn't.

Dulles' eyes were flashing between deep twitches. "Incidentally," he said, "I've been meaning to ask you— just how long *have* you been procuring women for the Shah of Iran?"

Dulles' teeth clicked like a thrift-shop typewriter as he watched me formulate my thoughts. Procuring women? A question that definitely demanded an answer. I said, "Sir, I do not *personally* procure women for the Shah of Iran."

His expression had turned into a question mark. He said, "Somewhere in your reply there seems to be a qualification."

"Well, I did, once, talk to a woman someone else had procured for the Shah, and . . ."

Dulles interrupted me, "What'd she say?"

"Do you want an exact quote?" I asked.

"Yes," he replied, his curiosity showing.

"'Cut, slash, and whooooooopeeeeeeeeeeeeeeeeeeeeee.'"

"What?"

"That's what she said."

"About the Shah?"

"About his, uh, technique."

"I see," he said, his eyes beginning to water with laughter that was not coming out. He was trying to look serious, and was not succeeding, as he asked, "Is that the only one?"

"Of the Shah's women?"

"Yes. That you know about."

"There was another one who said she had so much fun that she almost gave him half price."

Little red spots appeared on Dulles' cheeks as he pursued the conversation. "What was her price?"

"Three hundred dollars."

"That's pretty good," he said. "And Allen informs me that the Shah sleeps with lots of women."

"I'm not surprised."

His face became stern. "What do you mean you're not surprised?"

"I mean, I am not surprised that your brother told you that."

"What have you heard?"

"The word is that *every*body's trying to wire the Imperial Peacock bed."

"Good Lord."

"I know. But, after all, the Soviets gave Sukarno a 'take-along woman' before—or, so I hear—*we* could find a woman he wanted to take along . . ."

" 'Take-along woman'?"

"That's what they call it in some circles."

"I never heard of such a thing."

"Not many people have."

"No."

"It's just *one* way of putting it."

"I see. Is Allen mixed up in this?"

For a moment, I wondered if he was really seeking information about some of his brother's activities, or if he already knew the answers and was just trying to find out what I knew. I said, "I think some of your brother's people have been involved in, you could say, abetting the physical needs . . . of . . ."

"Hah! Abetting the physical needs. That's a good one!"

"Actually, I think what we're talking about here is local police and the like putting the finger on women for the Shah, Sukarno, some of the Saudis, a German . . ."

"Local police?"

"I think so."

"Think? You *think,* or you know?" He seemed upset.

"Think, sir," I replied soothingly.

"Hmmmmm. Sometimes it is better not to *know* too much. Think? Well, that's another matter."

"A fine distinction," I commented, not quite sure what he meant.

"You see," he said pensively, "Allen, for instance, *knows* many things that *I* only think."

"Yes, sir, well, these things happen."

"Harumph," he muttered and began rubbing his nose with his forefinger. "Are our State Department security people directly involved in any of this?"

"Do you want a *think* answer, or a *know* answer?"

"I see."

"Sir?"

"You've got the right idea. It's probably bad for me to know *or* think. Hah! Some people think I don't know much, and can't think anyhow. But, President Eisenhower asked me something along these lines once—women and such. I told him to talk to Allen. He asked me if Allen was responsible . . . for, uh, these women, and such. I told him again to talk to Allen, but that it really was not a question of responsibility. He said that it *had* to be a question of responsibility. He said that the whole point of government was making sure that the right people had responsibility, and that people with responsibility carried out that responsibility. I think that's the way he put it. Anyway, actually, there's considerable sense in what he says, but he recites it as if it's holy writ."

When Dulles said "Eisenhower," it came out as though he were bouncing the name off a newly hatched egg. He was careful. Ike had become part of the national furniture, and Dulles was well aware of it. And he talked a lot about Eisenhower's "sense of responsibility." Sometimes he seemed consumed with it. Of course, Eisenhower *did* have a great sense of responsibility, as well as a strong sense of position. I often thought that a sense of position weighed as heavily on Ike as his sense of responsibility. Sometimes, when I think about Eisenhower, I think of the story of Philip III of Spain who, so the story goes, died of a fever he contracted from sitting too long next to a burning brazier, because the person with responsibility for the removal of the brazier could not be found. Or, I think about the analysis of one of his ablest assistants, Bob Gray. Talking with Gray was always a pleasant challenge for my somewhat free-form head. *His* mind was more like a magnetic field that envelopes you. He said, "The thing about President Eisenhower comes down to paper—not too much paper, and, above all, the right paper. That's the trick, getting the *right* paper in front of him."

When I tried to get Gray to elaborate on what he meant by "right," he smiled and responded enigmatically. "If you know the President and you know the paper—I mean really *know*—then, instinct tells you how to match them up."

"Sort of like magic," I said.

"No," he replied crisply. "Hard work."

I saw a lot of Eisenhower during my years with Dulles, but a single frustrating Paris afternoon stands out in my memory. We were in and out of Paris all the time. This visit was for a NATO summit. I liked Paris. When I read recently that "three weeks in Paris can change a man's life forever," and I thought about all the changes, the twists, and turns in my life, I wondered just how much was due to Paris? Certainly my experience with Eisenhower that afternoon affected my view of "great men" forever. Beyond that, I am not sure. I had walked into the American Embassy residence looking for Dulles, who had spent the morning in the company of one of my security colleagues. Instead of finding Dulles, I was confronted by Eisenhower in a bathrobe, asking, "Where in *hell* is Foster?" I felt fear. The President's words seemed to tour the room on their own. The tension between us vibrated. I had taken a few hours off. Now, here I was, back on duty, facing an obviously angry and frustrated President of the United States. "*Goddamnit!*" he shouted. "Speak up! Where's Foster? I can't find Doug Dillon [C. Douglas Dillon was then U.S. Ambassador to France] or Foster or *any*body when I really *need* them."

I came to attention and attempted to rise to the occasion with the words, "The Secretary, Mr. President, must still be at the Quai d'Orsay [the French foreign office]."

Eisenhower was tense. Supposedly it is not possible to shake and be still at the same time, but Eisenhower was doing it. Frozen shakes. He seemed on the verge of exploding right through his skin. Then he started moving around the Dillons' lovely drawing room, going into something that resembled a Hopi snake dance. I couldn't believe it. He appeared near hysteria. I tried to hold down my fear. A crisis was at hand. He stopped the strange jumping moves and froze the shakes once again, and a peculiar pitch came into his voice—high and low at the same time—as he order-asked, "WHERE IN THE *HELL* DOES DOUG DILLON KEEP THE CHIVAS REGAL?"

I had always known that someday the President of the United States and I would do business. Here it was. I took action. I found him a bottle of Johnnie Walker. He dismissed it with, "I don't want any goddamn Johnnie Walker," and prowled the corners of the room muttering "damnit . . . damnit . . . damnit" and then got down on his knees to peer into the bottom of a cabinet. My head was beginning to feel as though somebody had picked it for a tennis rally, but I joined the President of the United States on the floor and found his face jammed into mine. He was growling like a bear gone berserk. I ducked when he sprayed out the words, "Where in HELL is that Chivas Regal?" and then we were crawling across the floor together to another cabinet when Ambassador Dillon appeared with—small miracle—a bottle of Chivas Regal. I couldn't get off my knees fast enough, but Dillon carried it off easily. Eisenhower slumped into a chair with his bottle, seeming very human. He thanked me for my "assistance" and Dillon mixed me a drink.

I liked Dillon. He was a nicely mixed compound of power, position, and common sense. Strangely enough, after that memorable encounter with Eisenhower, my meetings with Dillon, more often than not, seemed to relate to dead batteries. It got to the point that I was joking about what I called THE GREAT C. DOUGLAS DILLON BATTERY BREAKDOWN JINX. The first, and most remarkable, of those breakdowns occurred right there in Paris outside Maxim's and in front of Aristotle Onassis, who had been drinking heavily, and had taken on the look of a bloated Buddha. The Paris fog was wet, and lightning scribbled scary messages across the sky as we learned that the battery in Dillon's limousine had just died. The Dulleses, the Dillons, and I just stared at the wounded vehicle. Onassis, who, at the time, was trying to put through a deal to carry all Saudi Arabian oil in his tankers, was standing behind us, eyeing Dulles as though he was preparing to land and Dulles was the beach. Dulles looked over at him and some of the lightning seemed to flash between them as they eyed each other over the chasm of widely divergent lives. When one of my shoulders somehow found its way into the side of the Greek's neck, he jammed forward the bloated Buddha face—a living monument to his many pleasures—and whispered, "I am dangerous." Before I could reply, backfire sent us all into a crouch. This inspired me to find a taxi, and we left Onassis "singing" in the rain. It was close going.

Dillon and I were involved in other battery breakdowns with Dulles, including one right in the middle of New York City, but none was quite so dramatic as the one that night in front of Maxim's and Aristotle Onassis.

For a time, Dulles seemed to have dead batteries on the mind. He recalled stories of them to our aircraft commander on a flight to the Far East when, during a fueling stop at California's Travis Air Force Base, we noticed oil dripping from two of the old Constellation's four prop engines. I had questioned the plane's safety, to which the pilot indignantly replied that the Air Force was trying to make the old Constellations last "just a little longer" until "the big jets'll be ready." He boasted of his ability to "stretch these old birds out." I wanted to find another plane. But Dulles listened to the pilot, studied him intently, and then asked, "Are your batteries in good shape?"

This was probably the last question the pilot expected. His face sagged. His built-in military self-assurance vanished. "Batteries, sir?" he gurgled.

"Batteries," Dulles repeated, pronouncing it "bat-ries."

The pilot was now genuinely shaken. He said, "I assume they are fine, sir."

"Assume?"

"Yes, sir."

"You don't *know?*"

The pilot began to look intimidated. "Well, sir . . ."

Dulles waved him silent, saying, "I have had experience with dead batteries. On the ground. On the ground it is an inconvenience. In the air . . . it could be fatal."

"Yes, sir," the pilot agreed, looking incredulous as well as intimidated. "I'm sure all the batteries are fine."

"You say you're sure?"

"I'm sure, sir."

"Good. Then let's get on."

We did go on, spraying oil all across the Pacific, but with, I am sure, good batteries.

However, although this book may already seem to be turning into a trivia bombardment, I can assure you that there is more to it than losing batteries with C. Douglas Dillon and searching for whiskey with Dwight Eisenhower. As Dulles said to me one afternoon in San Francisco, during a conversation punctuated by the howls and bronchitic snorts of nearby foghorns, "When you look at history, you find that seemingly small events, character traits, eating habits can make the big difference, but," he went on, "history's clock never stops." His words came out like balloons popping between foghorn belches. When I looked questioningly, he added, "We've got to build bombs and try to get rid of them at the same time, and, the dickens of it is . . ." He stopped and pointed at some beatnik-looking people, asking, "*Who* are they?"

"Let's go," I said.

The San Francisco detective on my other side whispered in my ear, "What's the Old Man talking about— bombs, I mean?"

I think my reply had something to do with Halloween ending before Armageddon could begin.

2

In the Eye of Indira Gandhi

I had a dream about Indira Gandhi last year and awoke
in a sexual sweat remembering my meeting with her in
Delhi twenty-five years before, when her father, Jaw-
aharlal Nehru, was still alive and was Prime Minister. At
the time, I was going around the world with Dulles in my
best wash-and-wear suit.

India was a high point of the trip. I was excited, but our
landing at Delhi's Palam airstrip was rough, and I was
already sick. I had been told that India would be a spiritual experience, but, in Pakistan, just before Delhi, I had
acquired amoebic dysentery. From Mexican, *not* Pakistani
food. What was I doing eating Mexican food in Pakistan? I
am not altogether clear on that, but, any chance at a spiritual experience seemed, initially at least, to have been
destroyed. Great revelations have been known to come
from brain damage, rarely from dysentery. As we left the
aircraft, I looked up at the sky. It was yellow, like a crust

of bread. I almost stumbled into Dulles. My stomach and my mouth were on the verge of a joint effort. I was not prepared for the American Embassy security officer who came dashing through the clapping crowd, his voice at full tilt with startling news. "Jefferson! Jefferson!" he shouted, "*You* won't be riding with Secretary Dulles! Mr. Handoo, the Deputy Chief of Indian Intelligence has taken personal charge of the Secretary's security. *He* will be riding in the front passenger seat of the Secretary's car where I know *you* usually ride."

The man was in shock. His face said panic. I felt somehow to blame, although I didn't know why. There was heavy argument, shouting, all around me. My stomach wanted to go to ground. But, it was my job to ride with Secretary Dulles. I could not back down. Even so, I had to give them—the American security officer and Handoo—a way to save face. So, I held on to my stomach and let out a rebel "*Yeeeeeeeowwwwwwwwwwwww*" scream. It got their attention. I then announced, quietly, but in my "final position" tone, "I *always* ride here, up front, in the shotgun seat, with Secretary Dulles, in his car, but I'd be delighted to have this Mr. Handoo, whoever he is, and wherever he may be, ride *with* me, up front—he can sit in the middle—unless, that is, he is awfully, awfully big."

Handoo, as it turned out, was standing right there, listening. With a rich laugh, he rolled a tall, silver-thatched, and carefully arranged frame forward, held out his hand, and, his English touched by Oxford, said, "*I* am Handoo. Delighted to meet you. I accept your invitation . . . to the . . . shotgun seat—how colorful—I will even furnish a shotgun, if you wish. Perhaps we can go tiger hunting while you are here."

Tiger hunting? The tiger was already in my stomach. "With a shotgun?" I asked.

"No," Handoo replied, "the tiger would not understand the language of the shotgun."

Handoo later explained that by "tiger hunting" he meant holding a spear under a tree that held a tiger, in the expectation that when the tiger jumped, the unsuspecting beast would hit the spear. "That simple," he said. I never found the time, but, at the airport, I assured him that shotgun seat was merely a figure of speech and put him up front, between the driver and myself. I had extricated Dulles from the clutches of an Indian official who seemed to be trying to either kiss or smell the Secretary of State's hand with a nose as big as my fist, and we drove off the airstrip toward Delhi.

Handoo kept laughing. My vision was blurred. I looked back at Dulles, who was trying to communicate with the Indian official accompanying him. They both appeared to be choking to death. Janet Dulles, sitting between them, grabbed her husband's hand. He seemed reassured. The Indian stopped talking. They all smiled. My eyes wandered, beyond the road. I remembered an artist's conception of freeways between planets. For a moment I became convinced that *this* was the off-ramp to Mars. Perhaps it was the dysentery. More likely the clammy heat. Or both. The heat enveloped us like a cloak just hung out to dry. The sky had turned the color of pale vomit.

After a stop at the Rashtrapati Bhavan, palace of British proconsuls turned residence of Presidents of India and now temporary home for John Foster Dulles and party, we drove to Teen Murti, official residence of Prime Minister Nehru. The boulevards and buildings of New Delhi were impressive. Nearby, in Old Delhi, were the open drains, the bodies rotted by disease, the spoiled food. But, here, was splendor. As we drove, Dulles said, "They are all saying that I don't like Nehru. That is just not the point. He and I do not always operate on the same plane, but . . .

well, I am going to prove that you do not have to be celestial to get along with Nehru."

When they met, I thought Nehru was going to hand Dulles a flower. *That* would have been celestial. Dulles saw the flower first and angled himself around the Prime Minister, coming out on the other side, away from the flower. The flower went to an aide, who handed it to me. Dulles went with Nehru into the Prime Minister's study. Handoo took me and my flower into the garden where Nehru's pet panda—black, white, and wooly—was kept in a large net cage around a tree. "We had an American in that cage once," he laughed.

Not sure how to take his remark, I asked, "All you needed to hold him was that net?"

"Oh yes, the net was fine. The trouble was, he didn't get along with the panda."

"So, you took him tiger hunting," I said, trying to keep it light.

"As a matter of fact, we did," Handoo responded, diffidently, and strolled off, leaving me to admire the peach trees with their pale pink blossoms blowing in the warm, wet wind.

I wondered what was happening?

I was to wonder what was happening for quite some time. The meeting between Nehru and Dulles had been scheduled for fifteen minutes. Three hours later I was still looking at pandas and peach trees, and Dulles was still in Nehru's study.

It was hot.

The sun oozed a peculiar, pinkish red.

I asked for something to drink, and a servant poured me tea from a silver teapot so thinned by centuries of polishing that it could have been pierced, like rice paper, with a stiff forefinger.

I sipped the tea and rubbed my eyes. They were tired.

The light that confronted them was bright and hot. You could *see* the heat. The faces around me began to look like overexposed photos. One man, who always seemed to be near, reminded me of a hanging plant, all head and hair, in the air. Finally, an Indian Foreign Office official who had been "hover-running" around, looking worried (*importantly* worried), stopped his hovering, and stopped his running, and said, "I hope that this delay does not mean that war is breaking out!" His voice was flat, without ornament. It seemed to conceal an insult, but I couldn't be sure. His eyes—brown eyes, with a soft texture, like button mushrooms—told me nothing.

Irritated, I responded, "Maybe it means that *peace* is breaking out."

The man looked puzzled. The word "peace" does sometimes have that effect on people. It puzzles them. But, Indira Gandhi, standing nearby, overheard my remark and said, "Yes, yes, yes, you are quite right . . . we must think of peace . . . 'peace breaking out' . . . I like that. If we think enough of, concentrate on, peace, well, then, perhaps we will *have* peace, genuine peace, and not just the absence of war. Still, I suppose, we will always have our enemies." She paused, frowned, and, with no warning, asked me, "Are you armed?"

Indira Gandhi was staring straight at me. In 1956, she was a very beautiful woman, with large dark eyes that said they wanted to surface what they were hiding. I was transfixed. Her question seemed, somehow, to be wrapped in a bag of air, as if to shield it from the answer she was really looking for. I stuttered, "Yes, uh, ma'am. I am armed. Just as your people are when they come to the United States."

Her frown turned into a smile. It was like a cool kiss. She purred, "Of course," and touched my cheek with her forefinger. Then, in very British English, she murmured,

"You are so . . . *un*-American . . ." and floated away. I was not accustomed to being called "un-American" but noted in my diary, "Un-American from her was, I suppose, some sort of compliment. A fine strong woman. Something that eludes me." (I was reminded of that note ten years later, when Pennsylvania Senator Hugh Scott told me that Lyndon Johnson had said of Indira Gandhi, "For a woman, she's a hell of a leader, or, maybe, for a leader she's a hell of a woman, or . . . actually, when I met her, what I wanted to do was look under that damn wrap-around thing she wears, and check . . .")

Mrs. Gandhi disappeared into Teen Murti's inner recesses, leaving behind a delightful fragrance that, I decided, could only be very personal. Unlike Lyndon Johnson in the sixties, I had no doubts as to her womanhood.

Handoo returned. With a leer in his cultivated voice, he said, "The lady likes you."

"What does *that* mean?" I asked.

"Very little, I am afraid. But, then . . ."—he patted my shoulder—"who knows?"

"Does it make me safe from being locked up in the panda net?"

"Quite possibly," he whispered. Although he was still standing right in front of me, I felt that he was drifting away. I noted at the time that it was as if what was inside him was leaving what was outside of him. You couldn't see it, but you knew it was happening.

After watching his internal self "float away" for a minute, or two, I asked: "Me aside—do you only put Americans in there?"

"No, no," he laughed, seeming to return for a moment, "we are not partial to Americans in that regard."

Nehru and Dulles came up behind us, talking, Dulles

saying, "Yes, Prime Minister, we had our British experience, too, but it is not as 'fresh' as it is with you."

The Prime Minister nodded, helped Dulles into the car, and said, his tone indicating surprise, "You have understanding . . . yes, you do have understanding."

Handoo and I jammed ourselves into the front seat. I told him that I thought that Mrs. Gandhi was "very beautiful," and he replied, somewhat enigmatically, "In her eye lies power, and you are in her eye. Remember, she has been to jail, and her heroine is Joan of Arc."

Her eye? Jail? Joan of Arc? My mind wobbled.

Handoo got out before we reached the Rashtrapati Bhavan, and Dulles asked me, "Just *who* exactly *is* this Handoo fella?" When I told him that Handoo was "very high up" in Indian Intelligence, he had another question. "Who *else* does he report to—aside from Indian Intelligence, that is?" To my puzzled silence, Dulles said, "Handoo does not report to my brother, Allen . . . I don't think. Or, well, maybe he does. Lots of people report to Allen, and he doesn't know they report to him, or they don't know they report to him, or, both, or . . . strange business . . . intelligence. Strange. But, necessary, I suppose. People in this part of the world are very good at it. Invented a lot of it. But, *does* this fella report, do you know, to Allen . . . or, uh . . . the Soviets?"

I told him that, as far as I knew, Handoo did not report to the CIA, *or* the Soviets, or, for that matter, anyone else other than his Indian superiors—although, of course, one could never be absolutely sure.

Dulles snorted. "If he doesn't report to Allen *or* the Soviets, well, *that's* certainly unusual." Then, his eyes going from twitch to twinkle, he said, "I hear you made quite a hit with Mrs. Gandhi."

I reacted as if a mousetrap had snapped on my nose,

even to muttering, "Ouch!" before breathing the question, "Where'd you hear *that*, Mr. Secretary?"

Looking smugly secretive, he said, "Word gets around."

That was not a Dulles-type answer. I was confused. I asked, "Did Handoo tell you this?"

Dulles' chuckle became a cackle. "No. Perhaps he told Allen, though."

Without thinking it through, I said, "There hasn't been time."

The cackle went down deep into his stomach and came up a belch. "Allen loves to say that he is everywhere—not that I really believe *that*."

"But, Handoo . . ."

"If he told Allen, you'll hear from Allen."

"Sir, I don't *know* that Handoo talks to the CIA."

Dulles was enjoying himself. "Oh, of course, I'm not sure about that, either."

"Well . . ."

Dulles held up his hand. "She, Mrs. Gandhi, doesn't like us Americans too much, but"—the cackle was really deep and evil—"she seems to see something in *you*. And, some people speak to Nehru only through Mrs. Gandhi."

"What are you saying?"

"You have caught the eye of Indira Gandhi."

"She has nice eyes," I said, softly, and left him at his room in the Rashtrapati Bhavan.

Dulles' meeting with Nehru made big news, of sorts. One English language newspaper bannered, NEHRU, DUL-LES AGREE TO AGREE.

"How do you 'agree to agree'?" a security colleague asked me.

I replied with a question. "How do you get 'in the eye of Indira Gandhi'?"

It all started, I suppose, in early 1954. I was a twenty-six-year-old would-be poet, married with a baby son, so, although I was taking graduate seminars at Washington, D.C.'s George Washington University (G.W.U.), I definitely needed a job. The State Department, only three blocks from G.W.U., was perfect. But one day, while I was working in a small "intelligence" unit hidden away in an annex, my chief, a prince of a man named Bill "Bud" Uanna, blew into my run-down room and roared, "Have you ever been to the Secretary of State's office?"

There was none of the chrome of a James Bond novel about the scene. More the peeling plaster of John le Carré. The annex was a venerable apartment building, taken over by the State Department as a "temporary" during World War II. It had radiators that hissed and toilets that appeared in unexpected places, sending the sound of flushing right out through the walls and into the middle of discussions of "secret" intelligence matters. Sometimes the sound was comforting, giving assurance that the human condition was, after all, still just that, a human condition. Also comforting was the sense of seedy respectability, of secrets that were secret because nobody really wanted to know them. That, of course, was not altogether true—*some* of the secrets were desperately desired by others. Many others. Enemies. Friends. Superiors. Subordinates. "Secrets" you see, were what it was all about. Sometimes only the sound of flushing saved my sanity. But Uanna made no secret of his feelings as he repeated, "Have you ever been to the Secretary's office?" and added, "I need somebody to relieve Ellis."

Our job was to evaluate and summarize secret reports (in one box and out the other) and I was deep in the middle of a "hot" one when Uanna interrupted my concentration. Irritated by the distraction, I rose from my chair and bit out some words, "No, Bud, I have never been to the Secretary's office. I do not even know where the Secretary's office is. Who is Ellis?"

"Who's Ellis?" he screamed.

I feared for Uanna's blood vessels as I repeated, "Yes. Who, pray tell, is Ellis?"

"*The guy with the Secretary!* That's who." he shouted, continuing, "Security! The Secretary of State! He works for *me* now."

I sank back down into the chair. "Works for *you?* The Secretary of State? Works for you?"

"No!" He was really exasperated. "The guy *with* him works for me. His security officer. Under the new, the latest, reorganization, the guy—Ellis—works for me now."

"Oh. I understand," I responded, not understanding at all, but adding, "Have you met him? Ellis, I mean."

"No!" he bellowed. The tension was thick and expanding. He was speaking as if each word was being produced under some great inner pressure totally detached from the air passing through his larynx, as he continued, "No, I have not met the Secretary, either. I have talked to him on the phone—Ellis, that is."

"Hell of a way to run a government," I mumbled.

"What! You think this is funny?"

"Do I get five minutes of judo lessons before I go?"

"No time. Just *look* as if you *know* judo."

I hadn't been serious, but he was. "Look?" I asked.

"Sure," he said, getting ever more serious. "Pressed lips. Loose arms. *You* know."

"This is my training?"

"Right. You know how to shoot, don't you?"

"Yes. I do. So, okay, what do I do? Strap on a gun?"

"That's illegal."

"Illegal?" It was my turn to explode. In disbelief, I went

on, "How can it be illegal? I mean lots of people just plain don't *like* Dulles. Isn't the job to protect the guy?"

"*Yeah!*" Uanna erupted, again. "Right! Sure. Jeez, and errrrr, uh, uh . . ." Incoherence had set in. He was gargling his words, but, after a minute, his voice began to clear, and he said, more reasonably, "Look, *I* don't like *any* of this. I'm a fence man. An alarm man. A wire man. A lock man. Phones. Walls. You name it. But, protection! . . . Guns! Particularly guns. *Most* particularly guns when there are no guns. Or can't be guns. Or should be guns. Or . . . it's crazy. Just plain crazy. Okay? So, sure, Ellis *probably* does carry a gun. Sure. Maybe it's even his own gun. Jeez. How should I know? Maybe it's his father's gun. *I do not know.* I do not *want* to know. What I do know is that it is illegal at this point, and the point to that is that that is not the point. The *point* is that we gotta get somebody over there—Now!—to relieve the guy—Ellis!—for lunch. *That* is the point."

Uanna was a good man with a large heart and large frustrations. He was, in fact, a burglar-alarm expert. He loved burglar alarms like some people love flowers. He cherished them. All kinds of alarms, the wiring, everything. If alarms could grow, he would have grown them. Bodyguards were just not his "thing."

"Where do I go?" I asked, crisply.

"He chopped his words. "*The* . . . *Secretary's* . . . *office. New State Building.* Don't ask me *where* in the New State Building. Ask the guard at the door when you get there. Okay?"

I felt as though I were decomposing. Then, like magic, adrenaline surged. In an instant, I became fiercely determined to get out there and find the office of the formidable John Foster Dulles. Adventure beckoned. The flag flew. My Secretary of State needed me. He didn't know it, but I knew it and I also knew that I must stop talking and act.

Frenzied excitement mixed with fear hit me like a high-ball at seven in the morning, and, my words striking the air like tennis balls slamming into a vat of rice pudding, I said, "Bud, you are my chief, and I will do it! *I am on my way!*"

Uanna, his face preparing to explode from sheer spontaneous combustion, waved me out of the room.

Now, fully trained to be the Secretary of State's bodyguard, I approached the "New State" building armed with my pocketknife and wondering what mad planet of astrology had launched me on this course. The building guard at the entrance to the edifice called "New State" politely informed me that if I rode the elevator to the fifth floor, I would be unable to miss the office of the Secretary of State. I took his advice, and, sure enough, on the fifth floor, there it was, to my right—flags, seals, the works! I turned right, moved toward the flags, and found myself on my knees, seeing stars and holding my head, wondering why my eyes were closed when they were open and seeing stars. A deep voice was whispering in my ear, "You okay, son?" My eyes focused and followed the floor to the bottom of the glass wall that was so clean that I had not seen it before slamming into it. The deep whisper in my ear kept repeating, "You okay? You okay? You okay?" Arms were helping me to stand. The voice and the arms belonged to a man with a pronounced profile. At that moment, I could hardly see him between the stars dancing around my eyes, but I learned later that he was the Department's Counselor, Douglas MacArthur II, career diplomat and nephew of the famed general. I mumbled my thanks and, panting, hot, and hurt, I picked up my bruised ego and stumbled on toward the inner sanctum of John Foster Dulles. My training had not prepared me for dealing with glass walls.

Bewilderment overcame the bruised ego when I found

the mysterious Ellis in a small inner reception room behind the one with the glass wall. His instructions were
brief. They consisted of "Keep an eye on things, and, oh
yes, answer the phone if it rings." I waited for more, and,
when there was no more, I asked, "Is that all?"

"That's it," he replied.

"Shouldn't I meet Seretary Dulles?" I asked.

"You won't even see him," he said. "The man's not going
out."

"But," I asked, trying to get some fiber into my words,
"just suppose that he does?"

"He won't."

"Yes, but, just suppose."

"He is not going out."

"Yes, but . . ."

Ellis gave me a "Why didn't they send somebody else?"
look as he said, "Okay, he's not going out, but, if, just if,
he does, well, you get in this private elevator here and go
with him, and while you're riding down to the basement
where we keep his car, just, you know, introduce yourself."

"But . . ."

"Just keep an eye on things, answer the phone."

"That's really it?"

"That's really it," he concluded, and, after introducing
me to the Secretary's secretary, Phyllis Bernau, and Special Assistants Rod O'Conner and John Hanes, Ellis went
to lunch. Hanes told me some years later that when he
first saw me he wondered what high school they had let
me out of. Although I had turned twenty-six, I was often
taken for eighteen or nineteen. It bothered me.

However, I had my instructions, my training, everything, and, suddenly, I felt a great lurch of courage. It
lasted about thirty seconds. But, for that thirty seconds,
deep down in the private theater of my mind, I was Buf-

falo Bill, Jesse James, Billy the Kid, and General George Smith Patton all rolled into one. Then, I remembered. I did not have a gun. Euphoria turned into depression. I froze, staring at the outer door, questioning the sanity of a man—me!—who would put himself in such a position. The spell was interrupted by the appearance at the door of a French general with a chalk-white face and shaking hands. He didn't say anything. He just looked loudly into my eyes. Relieved to have something to do, I helped him off with his coat. His fingers were shaking individually, each at its own pace. He began to sink to the floor, and I held him up until Phyllis Bernau and the Chairman of the Joint Chiefs of Staff, Admiral Arthur Radford, escorted him into Dulles' office.

It was not until ten years later, when I was reading a book on Vietnam by Bernard Fall, that I realized that the shattered Frenchman was General Paul Ely, chief of the French general staff, just returned from Vietnam and in Washington to tell Eisenhower and Dulles that without an American air strike, Dien Bien Phu was lost to the Communists. He did not get the air strike, and, as Ellis had predicted, I did not even see Dulles that first day.

That's the way it started. Nearly five years and over 300,000 miles with John Foster Dulles. Life lived at full volume, although not without its static. And, as I told Indira Gandhi, I did, in time, carry a gun (the subject interested her to such a degree that she even asked one of Handoo's men where I carried it).

Actually, my experience with security, intelligence, and Washington chicanery prior to Dulles was a bit more extensive than I may have indicated. Indeed, just before my glass-crashing first day with—or, near—the Secretary, I had been trying to help the Secret Service and the FBI communicate with one another. It was difficult. In today's terminology, they just did not relate. The Secret Service's research chief at the time even went so far as to tell me, "The Bureau [the FBI] *hates* us. They just hate us. J. Edgar Hoover thinks *he* should be protecting the President, so, all of them—*all* of those FBI people—hate us, and we don't get their reports on dangerous characters who might go after the President, and they lock up our informants even when they know they are our informants—*especially* when they know they are our informants."

When I told him that my unit in the State Department got the FBI's reports on possible assassins and the like, his eyes filled with near religious fervor. When I added that I had good friends in the FBI, he clutched my shoulder, clawing, as if something was buried in it. His whispered "Ahhhhhhhh . . ." was orgasmic. Then, his voice barely making its way through the Washington humidity, he murmured, "Could you, uh . . . ?" I finished his question, ". . . give you . . . copies of their reports?"

"Yes! Oh, yes." He looked as Columbus would have probably looked if Columbus had really known what he was discovering.

"I could do that," I said.

"You will be doing a great and patriotic service."

"I'll be glad to help, but . . . hell . . . I can't believe the FBI *hates* you. I mean, that's crazy!"

"I know, I know," he said, sadly. "Some of my best friends, and all that, are FBI agents. But, the Bureau hates us."

"I see," I said, with a smile. "When *they* are they, *they* don't hate you. But, when *they* are *it*, they hate you."

"Are you trying to be funny?" he asked, looking hurt.

"I wonder if it's like this in Moscow?"

"Worse."

"That's good."

"What do you mean good?" He was indignant. "They're so screwed up that a KGB order to assassinate their own

President, or whatever he is, might come out as an order to assassinate *our* President, and then where would we be?"

"You can't be serious?"

"I am always serious." He was grim.

"Okay, sure. I'm just trying to understand what's going on. Relax. I will help you as best I can. Part of my job is to distribute summaries of those reports to 'cleared' people—people I think should see them. So, well, you *are* cleared aren't you?"

"Cleared?" He jumped. "Now, you've *got* to be kidding. Of course I'm cleared. I wouldn't have this job if I weren't cleared, would I?"

"Right. So, I'll send over the reports."

He jumped again. "No, no, no. It's not that simple. If the Bureau finds out you're giving us their reports, why, they'll cut you off! Fast! And they might come after you."

"Come after me?"

"In a manner of speaking."

What did I say to that? I said, "Some of *my* best friends really *are* FBI agents."

He smirked at my confusion. "You may need them."

"Okay," I said, "I will personally deliver the papers."

"Not here."

"Where?"

"You name it."

I thought for a moment and said, "Meet me tomorrow afternoon at, oh, four o'clock at—how 'bout Quigley's drugstore on the George Washington University campus? Three blocks from me. Six, or so, from you."

His eyes glittered as he said, "That's spooky."

"No. Convenient."

Thus did I become a fragile link between those two great services, the Federal Bureau of Investigation and the United States Secret Service. It remained relatively simple until a CIA operative of my acquaintance confronted me with, "We *know* you're passing FBI 'secrets' to the Secret Service."

Caught in the Act! For a short minute I felt guilty, like a traitor, or something. But traitor to who? Wasn't I just trying to make my own government work better? Wasn't that a part of being a public servant? To make the government work better? Even the 'secret' government, or whatever you wanted to call it. In truth, wasn't I a patriot? I said to the CIA operative, as he stared accusingly at me, "The Secret Service *needs* the information if they are going to do their job of protecting the President properly. It's that simple."

"I know," he said, seeming to agree. "*We* don't like the FBI, either."

Irritated, "It has nothing to do with liking, or not liking the FBI. I *like* the FBI. I like the Secret Service. I even like you. It's just a matter of a breakdown in communications. I am trying to help, and, besides, *we* have to *work* with the Secret Service! They are important to us. My God, we all do work for the same government, don't we?"

"Now, now," the Agency operative said, in his best dealing-with-puppy-dog voice, "we just want your help."

"'We'? The CIA?"

"Of course."

I got mad. Really mad. "Are you trying to blackmail me?"

"No, no," he said soothingly. "It's just that we understand that J. Edgar Hoover has a file on our Director, Allen Dulles, and *we* want it!"

"What's that got to do with me?" I asked.

"Well, you seem to be able to, uh, find your way to FBI, uh, information, and, well, your position does seem a bit compromising."

I was incredulous. "It sounds like what you're saying is

that if I don't try to steal a file from J. Edgar Hoover himself, you will tell the FBI that I am passing their reports to the United States—repeat, United States—Secret Service. Is that what you are saying?"

"Let's not be crude."

"Let's not be ridiculous."

"Think about it."

I really bristled. "I don't have to think about it."

"You would be doing a patriotic service."

"Save me!"

"What?"

"You wouldn't understand."

Suddenly, he became very prim, "I certainly understand patriotism."

"Maybe you don't understand *my* brand of patriotism," I said, a little bewildered with the whole turn of the conversation.

"Patriotism is not subject to individual definition."

"We aren't getting anywhere here."

"Just think about what I've said."

I worried about it, but I didn't think about it, and I never heard from the guy again, but, two years later, I did tell Secretary Dulles about it. His reaction was, "What could Hoover have on my brother?" Shortly thereafter he had me tell the story *to* his brother, who listened, and coughed, and said, "Hoover's an old fox, but I know how to tree a fox."

I just nodded, but the Secretary grunted out, "Allen, if you ever tree J. Edgar Hoover, he'll have you right up in that tree with him, and the dogs barking at the bottom of the tree will be *his* dogs."

Allen Dulles rolled his brother's response around in his mind and then fumbled out the words, "Edgar's done some . . . good . . . necessary . . . things. Valuable man.

Useful. Still, something strange there . . . can't quite get next to it."

It sometimes seemed to me as if Allen Dulles regarded J. Edgar Hoover as the wrong wall for the right pictures, although you could never really be sure with Allen Dulles. For that matter, you could never really be sure with J. Edgar Hoover. They both came out of that dark underside of the world that somebody has described as being like a "trading company of bodies and souls." And, in my years with Foster Dulles, I inhabited a small corner of it, a corner where the name of Indira Gandhi kept popping up.

During a trip to Miami, a year or so before the visit to Delhi, a local detective who had been "acquiring" (his word) women for the Shah of Iran told me that the Shah had "boasted" that he had "had" just about every woman "worth having" in his part of the world except Indira Gandhi. Still somewhat naive about these matters, I responded, "The Shah doesn't really 'play around,' does he? I mean, he's married, isn't he?"

The Miami detective groaned. He rubbed some snuff (I think it was snuff) on his gum, and said, "To say that the Shah doesn't play around is like saying that Hitler died for our sins."

I bought him a drink and wondered who Indira Gandhi was. I found out in Delhi, and, after that, her name kept cropping up in my life.

Many years later (around 1974) I was in San Francisco doing public relations for the Environmental Protection Agency, when an Indian Public Health official came through seeking the obligatory "briefing" on matters polluted. He was very serious, wanting to talk of change, noting that, for India, revolution was but a small shift in the "emphasis" of suffering. I listened for a while, and then asked him about Handoo. He shuddered, and gurgled,

"Ahhhhhhhhhhhh . . . the eye . . . eeeeeee . . ."

"The eye? Of Mrs. Gandhi?" I whispered, fearing for a moment that I might hear my own words.

His face seemed to shrink, like one of those shrunken heads you see in a museum. His words spattered, dripped, like an egg thrown against a wall, as he said: "Ohhhh . . . Yes. The eye of Mrs. Gandhi. How did you know?"

"I have been told," I said, looking straight at him, "that I am in the eye of Indira Gandhi."

The man shivered.

I shook.

We were interrupted by the ring of my phone. It was a lady in Chico, California. She announced that she had seen a strange and very dead cow in her backyard, and she told me, in no uncertain terms, that it was most certainly the responsibility of the United States Environmental Protection Agency to have that cow removed. I suggested that she contact her local public health office and found myself listening to a lecture on the use of taxpayers' money.

When I finally hung up, the Indian Public Health official, who had heard my end of the conversation, appeared terrified as he posed the question, "It is now your responsibility to bury dead cows?"

"Not sacred cows!" I wisecracked.

I was wrong to wisecrack. The poor guy's eyes were popping out of their sockets. But, his voice was cast iron as he said, "You are no longer in the eye of Indira Gandhi."

3

The Kitchen Freeze, "Mommie Dearest," and Other Affairs Nuclear, Diplomatic, Romantic, and Satanic

Dulles had jammed himself into a kitchen corner in New York's Waldorf Towers and was shouting into a telephone, "If *we* don't test nuclear weapons in the atmosphere, and the *Soviets* don't test nuclear weapons in the atmosphere, then, it seems pretty obvious, there won't be much radiation in the atmosphere!"

When he hung up, he mumbled, "The military [he pronounced it "millinary"] can be very inflexible . . . it's their strength, and, at the same time, their weakness . . . and they've got *'surrounding'* their civilian leaders down to a fine art, although, I must say . . . Ha! . . . some of my best friends are in the 'millinary.' "

"Did you say 'surrounding,' sir?" I asked.

"Yes. They get their civilian leaders into these fancy airplanes and then they get them flying 'round and 'round with a lot of salutes and strong coffee and . . ."

"Strong coffee, Mr. Secretary?"

"Yes. Spirits, too, of course."

"You mean booze?"

"Booze, yes." Dulles chuckled. "And bugles."

"Booze and bugles? Our civilian defense leaders are corrupted with booze and bugles?"

"I didn't say corrupted," he said, turning stern.

"Well, influenced. That's really something. Booze, bugles, and strong coffee."

"And airplanes," he added, with a large twinkle.

"Round and round . . ."

"That's right. Of course, I don't really blame anybody in this, and, when you think about it, sometimes the 'millinary' themselves are, in some ways, easier to deal with, than their civilian masters . . ."

"Flying round and round with their booze, bugles, and strong coffee," I finished for him.

He laughed. "Well, bugles and strong coffee are all right, I guess, if they help us to keep the peace."

"Booze?"

"Another subject."

"What about Old Overholt rye?"

"That's *my* drink," Dulles said, with finality.

"Ambassador [Henry Cabot] Lodge says that if he ever becomes Secretary of State he'll be able to afford 'little eccentricities' like drinking Old Overholt, too."

Startled, Dulles asked, "Did he really say that?"

"Yes, sir, Mr. Secretary, he did."

"To you?"

"Yes."

"Lodge lacks the stamina."

"For Old Overholt?"

"No, to be Secretary of State." [He pronounced secretary "sekertary"].

I laughed. Dulles didn't. I said, "If the world could hear the way you've been talking for the past few minutes, everybody'd be singing that song, 'I'm in Love with John Foster Dulles' or is it 'I Made a fool of Myself Over John Foster Dulles'?"

His look was strange. Almost a pout. "They're actually *playing* that thing on the radio, aren't they," he asked and paused, before adding, "It kind of makes fun of me, doesn't it?"

"Mr. Secretary," I responded, "you are one of those rare happenings—a legend in your own time."

Dulles guffawed. "President Eisenhower's the legend. I just carry some of the excess baggage."

The whole thing seemed to depress him, and I tried to pull him out of it with, "I haven't heard any songs called 'I Made a Fool of Myself Over Dwight David Eisenhower.'"

"No, well, I wasn't the Allied Supreme Commander during World War II."

"*He* wasn't senior partner at a great international law firm like Sullivan and Cromwell."

Thoughtfully, Dulles murmured, "You know, it's funny, but that sort of thing really does impress the President. The 'Wall Street lawyer' business. Not my writing of the Japanese Peace treaty—which I regard as my most significant accomplishment—or my early role in a bipartisan foreign policy, but, no, what really impresses him is the Wall Street lawyer business. People accuse me of being too much the Wall Street lawyer, but I sometimes think that if I was more the Wall Street lawyer than I am, I'd be, well, closer to the President."

I thought about that. Closer to the President. I thought about the night we had flown down to Thomasville, Georgia, so that he could report to the President at Treasury Secretary George Humphrey's plantation and shooting preserve.

It was a cold night, even as far south as Thomasville,

but we were whisked from the airport to Humphrey's nearby establishment in a well-warmed limousine. Eisenhower was playing bridge when we arrived, but interrupted his game to closet himself with Dulles. We had made arrangements to spend the night in Thomasville at a place improbably called the Three Toms Inn. When one of the Secret Service men with the President asked me why Dulles was staying at the Three Toms with "all us peons" instead of "here at the plantation," I told him that it was quite simple, that "Dulles was not invited."

The agent, showing disbelief, asked, "How come? Dulles *is* a big New York lawyer, isn't he?"

The man's eyes bored into me, and I said something like, "Right now Dulles is Secretary of State, and maybe Ike doesn't like Secretaries of State."

"My, God, man," the agent snarled, his eyes now pushing me right back into the wall, "Ike *made* Dulles Secretary of State."

"Well," I said, "maybe Secretary Humphrey doesn't want him around here."

The agent laughed. "Humphrey *is* definitely king around here."

"But Ike's the President."

"That's right, and around here it's sort of like one king visiting another king."

This agent's not all blood and guts, I thought. He's a philosopher. I said, "And Dulles . . . in New York he was a king, but in Washington, and particularly in Thomasville, Georgia, he's just the Secretary of State, not fit for the manor, destined only for the Three Toms Inn."

"I think maybe you are getting close," the agent responded, with an evil chuckle.

That conversation was never finished because Dulles came out. He and I went straight into Thomasville and the Three Toms. Happily, I had a bottle of Old Overholt rye in my briefcase, along with official papers, ammunition, a blackjack, phone directories, his favorite detective stories, and a false mustache, which I knew I would never wear, but which gave me a laugh every time I looked at it. After we checked in, he suggested we break out the Old Overholt in his room. As I dug down into my briefcase, Dulles spotted the mustache, pointed, and asked, "*What* is that?"

I pulled the false mustache out, held it up, and said, "In case I ever have to disguise myself."

Dulles' laugh could have been a "ho, ho, ho" coming from a horse as he asked, "Disguise yourself so people won't know you're with *me?*"

"No, sir," I replied. "Actually, it's in case you decide you don't want people to know *you* have *me* with you."

Sadness crept into his look as he said, "The way some people talk about me, I'm the one who'll probably need the disguise."

"You do have your critics."

"Yes. So many people don't understand the difference between being willing to fight, if necessary, and wanting to fight. Yet, the surest road to war is to let your opponents think you do not have the will to fight."

I poured the whiskey and watched him sit down on the edge of a squeaking old bed, coatless and tieless, sipping Pennsylvania rye on the rocks and sniffing the smell of bad disinfectant that permeated the room. Tension, fatigue, and frustration showed in his sagging gothic features as he peered at me through those heavy spectacles. In spite of the rye, his voice was dry, like dust, with that persistent touch of the pulpit in it. His eyes twitched. Behind the twitch, they burned. I wrote in my notes at the time, "I'm worried about the man." And I recall wondering, in one of those odd mental flashes, if John Calvin drank rye whiskey, as I listened to Dulles talk about "strain" and "endurance" and "sacrifice." Pent-up feelings came spitting out. I prepared myself for a sermon. Instead, the rye rinsed his mind of its troubles, and his eyes twinkled as he chuckled out, "The radiators in this place sound as though they're ready to explode. Do you think I'm safe here?"

"Maybe we ought to move your bed away from the radiator," I said, trying to continue what I thought was a joke.

He took it seriously. "Good idea."

"Sir?" I questioned.

"That thing's full of boiling water, isn't it?"

"Steam."

He snorted. "A fine distinction."

My eyes surveyed the room. It was small, so small that, at best, I decided, we might get the bed eight, maybe ten feet from the radiator. "Do you want to move it?" I asked.

"Yes," he replied, "but let's have another drink first."

We had another drink and then moved the bed—screeching and scraping it across the floor for about five feet. He studied it for a moment, and then, looking satisfied, said, "That will do it."

I felt like saluting. Instead, I fixed us another drink, while Dulles sniffed around the room. He reminded me of a hound confused by too many scents.

Dulles had an aura of power as well as the pulpit about him. For most of his adult life he had been a man of great affairs, a participant in great events, living in the rarefied atmosphere of those whose everyday work has its effect on large numbers of people. It was a world of richly paneled partners' rooms, of elegant private clubs with the hallmark of enormously expensive simplicity, of town houses and country homes, a world of certainty, confidence, and continuity. However, the radiator's hiss, the rattling windows, and the smell of disinfectant seemed quite literally to put him in a different place both mentally as well as physically. Back on the edge of the newly positioned bed, stirring his drink with his forefinger, nose twitching, he announced, "The President and I *are* close, but . . . we aren't friends."

My mind rattled with the windows. "Sir?" I quacked.

"Your voice sounds funny," he said.

"It's just that, well," I stuttered, "you and the President *are* . . . friendly . . . aren't you?"

"Oh, sure, I guess we're friendly. Of course we are. Friendly enough to get the job done, certainly." He smiled at my confusion, and went on, "I guess I was just thinking of how close he is to George Humphrey."

"You mean he's closer to Secretary Humphrey than he is to you?"

"On a personal basis, yes."

I told him about my conversation with the Secret Service agent and he asked for another drink, worked his forefinger around in it, seeking the desired color and texture, and murmured, "The President of the United States *is* a modern-day king."

"What about Secretary Humphrey?"

"Well, as your Secret Service friend said, around *here*, I guess he's a king, too."

Dulles talked of many things that night. He had just briefed the President on the Suez Canal crisis. The frustrations and pain of "going against old allies like Britain, France, and Israel" were much on his mind. At one point, his voice strident, he said, "We *must* do *something—something!*—to limit the spread of nuclear weapons!" Then he began talking of Eisenhower's popularity and declared that he, Dulles, had not become "Sekertary" of State to "seek public acclaim." When I mentioned the Chinese, he rolled some rye around his mouth and said, "The Chinese have ancient skills in diplomacy and negotiation. They are skillful in reading an adversary's intentions. They have had thousands of years of experience and are always looking for signs and signals."

"The Communist Chinese probably don't like the signals they get from you," I remarked, lightly.

He didn't laugh. He said, "My signals don't bother the Chinese as much as they do some of our business people who want to do business with them." At that point I tried to put my drink on the hissing radiator and the glass slipped, splashing its contents up into the steamy hiss, sending the smell of incinerated whiskey into the air to mix with the disinfectant. Dulles roared, slapped his knee with the palm of his hand, and almost fell off the bed, dropping *his* drink in the process. The room began to smell like a tropical distillery. I picked up the unbroken glasses from the rag rug that partially covered the floor. Dulles said, "Pour us another, Lou."

"Mr. Secretary," I protested, "I think I've had enough."

"Well, let me have another jigger."

I poured for both of us and walked to the window. He followed me. We looked out at frost and naked tree limbs coming up at us like arthritic fingers, ghosts in the winter night. There was a knock at the door. I opened it and was confronted with a large, solid-looking haystack of a woman wearing the reddest lipstick I had ever seen. My first thought was, "My God, the caricature of a call girl." But she was no caricature. She was the real thing. I knew it when she looked past me, saw Dulles, and said, "Oh, Jesus, I never had a fish like him before. I don't know if I can handle it."

"Look, miss," I said, "I think you have the wrong room."

She pulled a slip of paper from her purse, looked at it, and said, "You're right. What a drag."

I smiled benevolently and eased the door shut. Dulles asked, "Was she what I think she was?"

"I believe so."

"Was she talking about me?"

"I think that what she was saying, when she saw you, was that you would have been beyond her previous experience."

"Well, she's certainly beyond mine."

"Yes, sir."

He sat down on the bed again, and said, "This is an *unusual* place."

"You mean the woman?" I asked.

"The woman, the radiator, this bed . . ."

When he said "this bed," it finally hit me why he wasn't anxious to sleep. He had back trouble, and the bed sagged. On trips abroad, we carried a bed board, but we didn't have a bed board in the Three Toms Inn. He looked dejected, and I knew he was bone tired. He seemed to want to talk, but, instead, was making odd little clucking sounds in his throat. To make conversation, I said, "Mr. Secretary, this crisis at Suez, the pressure on the Israelis to withdraw from Suez, and the criticism you're getting from the American Jewish community—your visit with the Israeli Ambassador just before we came down here—it all must be getting you down."

His forefinger, which had been vigorously blending the mud-colored tap water with the rye, moved from the drink to the side of his nose, which he started rubbing with a circular motion. It is not easy to stir your nose, but Dulles was trying as he responded, "It's ironic, isn't it? A lot of the Arabs have always regarded me as pro-Zionist, which, in a way, I suppose I always have been, but, now some people are calling me anti-Semitic, dredging up old trash from my Senate campaign in New York. It's crazy."

"You certainly aren't anti-Semitic."

"No. I told President Eisenhower that I'm being called anti-Semitic, and he said 'better you than me.'"

"Did he really say that?" I asked, finding it hard to believe.

"Of course, he did," Dulles snapped, looking unhappy. "The President's humor often takes a . . . practical turn."

Still startled, I said, "It is funny, though, that even the British are saying that you are anti-Semitic, anti-Israel. It's particularly ironic coming from the British, who didn't exactly help the founding of the State of Israel."

"That's the word, all right. 'Ironic.' Particularly because not only did they cause all kinds of problems at the beginning, but, after the end of the first Arab-Israeli war, they did everything they could to keep the Arabs stirred up against Israel. Kept the pot boiling. Classic British diplomacy. Divide and rule. Typical. Anything to keep their influence with the Arabs paramount."

This was news to me, and I tried to keep him going by asking, "Were they trying to keep Soviet influence out?"

He belched before answering. "They were trying to keep *our* influence out." He paused, shifting his finger to the other side of his nose. Then he continued. "They—the Labour government at that time—were trying to keep Israel weak because they were afraid that, unlike the Arabs at that point, Israel would take an independent course if she became strong and dominant. And then the Arabs would see that they could, like Israel, tweak the Lion's tail with impunity, which, of course, they had already seen, anyway . . ."

"Doesn't sound too sensible, really," I commented, trying to digest what he was saying.

"Harumph!" he grunted. "Conditions change. Times change. British diplomacy—never!"

"So, *they* are statesmen, and you are an anti-Semite."

He grunted again. "If they were called anti-Semitic,

they'd probably say it was all just part of the 'white man's burden.'"

"Hypocrisy."

"Of course." He looked down at the funny rug and was thoughtful. His finger was back in what was left of his drink.

I waited a minute, watching him, and then asked, "Did you know that we almost didn't land to fuel in Saudi Arabia last year, on the way to the Karachi SEATO conference, because your secretary, Phyllis Bernau, is Jewish?"

He looked puzzled. "What do you mean?"

"Just before we landed—it was after midnight and you were asleep—the Air Force stewards went a little berserk hiding booze under dirty clothes . . ."

Dulles remarked, incredulous, "Under dirty clothes!"

"That's right. They even wanted your Old Overholt out of my briefcase."

"To put under dirty clothes?"

"Well, they pulled a dirty sock over it and stuffed it into an old combat boot."

"Good Lord."

"They said the Saudis wouldn't let us land with booze aboard."

"Ridiculous."

"Yes, sir. And then one of them said, 'Thank God we don't have any Jews aboard, or they'd *never* let us land.'"

Dulles' face went from brownish red to pinkish purple. He snarled, "Ri . . . *dic* . . . u . . . *lous!*"

"That's right. Yes, sir. So, I said, 'Miss Bernau is Jewish,' and I thought that they'd both have heart attacks on the spot."

"Awful."

"Right. So, I told them to shut up, calm down, and let the pilot land the plane, but they kept on and I had to get a little intimidating."

"What do you mean intimidating?"

"Well, one of them said the Saudis might bring a 'whole army' aboard and asked me what I would do. I told him that I'd just have to shoot them all, but that I'd probably have to shoot him first and I really didn't want to do that because he was a nice fellow. Actually, basically, both stewards were nice fellows, but they were totally shaken."

Dulles' eyes glittered. He was very much awake as he said, "Unbelievable. And I slept right through it."

"You had your bed board."

"I certainly don't have it here."

"I know."

"When we landed there—you didn't have any trouble, did you?"

"Of course not. I wouldn't have stood for it. The Saudis were perfectly correct. But, it was touch and go for a time."

He frowned. "Was Phyllis asleep, too?"

"Yes, she was."

"Did you tell her about it?"

"No," I replied. "I may tell her sometime, but I don't know. She's such a neat little lady, and, well, I guess I don't want to, uh, needlessly disturb her."

"Yes. She's remarkable. My Lord, these ancient antagonisms! Bernie Baruch told me once that being Jewish was like having to wear special glasses that gave what you saw a particular shape. But, Phyllis—remarkable, so cheery, bright, loyal. I really don't know what I'd do without her."

Phyllis Bernau *was* remarkable, a delightful young woman who fell in love with one of Dulles' favorite assistants, Ambassador William B. Macomber. She is now Mrs. Macomber, but, at the time, I sometimes felt like the net in a game of tennis as they lobbed emotional balls at each other. Long flights to every part of the world brought on long conversations with her about the intricacies of the mind and the heart of William Macomber. It was sort of like dissecting the workings of a foreign power, and, indeed, while Dulles would be in one cabin trying to determine what made China work, she and I would be in another trying to determine what made Macomber tick. Macomber was brilliant and a fine human being. He was also volatile—amazingly and, sometimes, amusingly, so. I can recall, for example, entire minutes when I was convinced that he was living right out at the edge of his voice. The same trip that took us to India also found us winding our way through a funeral procession in Colombo, Ceylon. It was filled with orange-robed mourners, and firecracker throwers that drove Macomber into a near frenzy. We were trying to "rush" Dulles into the Embassy from the airport for a "secret" briefing, but every time a firecracker would go off, I would yell at the driver to speed up, and Macomber would yell at me, and I would yell at the driver, and Macomber's voice would almost leave his voice, and . . . it was wild. My affection and admiration for him were immense, but sometimes he got to me, and he will always be intertwined in my mind with that brief visit to Ceylon. When we finally succeeded in depositing Dulles in the Embassy, Macomber cornered me and a security colleague, and instructed us to "debug the room immediately." He added, "This meeting's gotta be *secret!*"

I was already unnerved by a furtive little character who, after telling my fellow security officer and me that he was "Intelligence" and that the local government was in his "back pocket," had us meet him down the hall by the water fountain. When we got to the water fountain, he whispered "Everything is in good order" and disappeared. I tried to get a drink of water, but the fountain didn't work, and, one week later, the government the "Intelligence" man had boasted of having in his "back pocket" fell to anti-American forces. Anyway, after Macomber barked his orders, I asked my colleague if he knew the whereabouts of our debugging equipment.

"It doesn't work," he informed me.

I had forgotten. Despite its reputation for dark deeds, the State Department Security Office at the time didn't have enough money to buy equipment that worked. Even if it had, we wouldn't have known how to use it. But, trying to look wise, as if we knew exactly what we were doing, we started running the "sweeper" over the walls. Suddenly, like an erratic volcano, Macomber erupted again, shouting that we *had* to find a certain briefcase that might be on the aircraft. He quickly formed up a posse that consisted of the State Department's top officials and me, and within minutes we were all in the well-guarded plane's 100-plus-degree hot cabin, burrowing our way through piles of briefcases, baggage, notebooks, and papers. Sweat streamed off everybody, and shirts began to come off. One very distinguished Assistant Secretary pulled off his trousers. Macomber exhorted us to ever greater effort. I felt as if I was in the middle of some bizarre, visual joke. At one point, Doug MacArthur murmured through pouring perspiration, "Thank God nobody is taking a picture of this. There are those who would say that their worst fears of how United States foreign policy is arrived at were confirmed. Ha! If the Russians and the British could only see us now!"

Macomber gave MacArthur a dirty look. But his words were polite as he said, "Doug, this is serious. Besides, if the British were in our shoes, they'd just quietly forget they lost the damn thing, and the Soviets, well, they probably wouldn't have lost it in the first place, but if they had, they'd just pretend it never happened, and, goddamnit, we're Americans, and we've gotta find that briefcase."

When somebody kicked a *Life* magazine to the floor and

it opened to a picture of Joan Crawford, I stopped Macomber in his verbal tracks with, "I wonder if Joan Crawford has the Secretary's picture in her bedroom?"

MacArthur leered through his own question, "Why should she do that?"

"Well," I replied, "she made a pass at him at '21' in New York."

Somebody snickered, and said, "Dulles probably wouldn't know what to do with her."

To which Carl McCardle, Dulles' irreverent press and public affairs chief—a rumpled laundry bag of a man, but nice—snorted, "You kiddin'? The Old Man'd shake her to her shoes."

"You mean she'd do it with her shoes on, Carl?" I asked.

"With Joan Crawford, you better believe it!" McCardle fired back.

I couldn't resist the question, "Carl, where did you get this, uh, intimate information?"

"I haven't *always* been in the State Department!" McCardle scoffed.

MacArthur huffed in with, "Lou, did she *really* make a pass at John Foster Dulles?"

"Sure," I replied. "He was just sitting there eating shrimp just flown in from Ireland . . ."

"*Shrimp* just flown in from *Ireland?*" McCardle blurted, drooling through his sweat. He liked to brag about his global stomach and the copious quantities of food he had consumed "from the shores of Tripoli to Wheeling, West Virginia." Years later, a favorite cousin of mine who is a Wheeling, West Virginia, reporter, Kitty Jefferson Doepkin, told me that Carl, who had been raised near Wheeling, would sometimes come home and "eat his way halfway through Wheeling, drink his way through the other half, and then eat his way right back through the whole town again, and nobody could figure out how he

got with Dulles—he just didn't seem to fit." He *didn't*
seem to fit and that, I think, was a great part of his attrac-
tion for Dulles. Dulles would look at Carl McCardle's
suede shoes, yellow shirts, and purple ties and see something he didn't see very often, and he liked it.

I looked through the thick, humid air at McCardle's
drooling, and said, "That's right, Carl, he was eating
shrimp from Ireland with the British Foreign Secretary . . ."

"They don't like the British Foreign Secretary in
Ireland," McCardle snickered, as he removed his yellow
shirt.

"No, but they do at '21,'" I responded, continuing. "And,
anyway, they were sitting there eating Irish shrimp when
Joan Crawford came sweeping in and leaned over Secretary Dulles, practically dunking her . . . bosom? . . ."

"Tits!" McCardle corrected.

"Right," I agreed. "And, so, there she was, practically
dunking them—and they were impressive—in the Secretary's shrimp sauce and she was breathing deeply, and
her perfume was *powerful,* and when he tried to stand up
she sort of slid into him . . ."

"Slid . . . into . . . him . . ." MacArthur whispered.

"Right," I said, "and there was an embrace, and . . ."

"Hey, now . . ." McCardle breathed.

"Get serious, people," Macomber growled. "We've *got* to
find that damn briefcase. There is a paper in there that
the Secretary absolutely *must* have!" He was doing his
job, keeping us on the track.

Actually, Macomber was magnificent. He got things
done, not for himself, but for Secretary Dulles. Even so,
the scene in that parked plane was surreal, and hot. It was
an oven. Macomber might have been a field marshal in
hell. We were all dripping with sweat, taking clothes off,
hurling briefcases at each other, putting clothes back on,

drinking stale water the plane had taken on somewhere west of Suez. Living Dada. Macomber kept churning around and around. McCardle got into "Dulles as Hollywood Love Target." MacArthur announced his fervent hope that his dear friend, the Permanent Undersecretary of the British Foreign Office, would "never find out about this little caper of ours."

Eventually, the missing briefcase, with its missing paper, or something resembling it, was found. Later that afternoon, after a short elephant ride, the Ceylonese police took me to a Buddhist shrine in an old Victorian house, thinking that I wanted to pray. It was a real, "working" shrine, full of rose petals and little girls kneeling, but, in fact, all I really wanted to do was hide for a time from elephants, American "Intelligence" agents, missing papers, and machinery that did not work.

Later, on the plane, I told Dulles of the adventures that had occurred while he was conducting United States foreign policy in Ceylon. He was wrapped in a polka-dot bathrobe, toying with a nightcap, jiggling the ice with a freckled forefinger. Mrs. Dulles sat nearby. His gaze wandered to the vacant window. There was that look at the back of his eyes, the inner tension, the coiled spring. He kept jiggling the ice with his finger. Finally, he said, "Bill Macomber sometimes seems like a bull in a china shop, but he doesn't really break much china." The Secretary laughed, releasing the tension, and added, "Besides, Bill gets things done. It's wonderful the way he gets things done."

"He's dedicated to you, sir."

"Yes, I believe he is," Dulles said, thoughtfully. "Actually, the thing about Bill is he is genuinely dedicated to the interests of the United States."

"More than his own, you mean."

"Yes. Exactly. Oh, he's ambitious. Wouldn't be any good

if he wasn't. But, he's an old-fashioned patriot, too. And his efforts—gargantuan efforts—haven't become his goal. They are still the way, not the end. Not too common these days."

"You are fortunate to have Bill and Phyllis, both."

"I know, I know . . . Phyllis is so efficient, so cheerful, so . . . so, so . . ."

"Womanly?"

"That's the right word. Thank heavens I don't inspire fear in everyone."

"Carl McCardle says you're a 'Hollywood Love Target.' "

The paperback detective novel Janet Dulles was reading fell to the aircraft's floor. She asked, "Did Mr. McCardle really say that?"

"He sure did," I replied.

"Well," she said, "Carl McCardle is sometimes given to overstatement, but . . . love target?"

Dulles added, seriously, "Actually, it's really too late for all that."

Janet Dulles looked at her husband and went "Tut, tut, tut."

I said, "Carol Burnett is becoming famous singing 'I Made a Fool of Myself Over John Foster Dulles' all over the place."

Dulles pinched his nose. His words came out like stones dropping into a pond. "Well . . . *that* . . . does . . . seem, well, foolish."

Janet Dulles giggled and said, "Allen would love it if somebody would write a song like that about *him*."

Dulles didn't laugh. His face twitching, he murmured, "My brother is . . . different . . . which is not to say that he does not like women."

Which brings to mind the morning America's master spy came through the private elevator door like a venerable old motor vehicle coming off a high-speed freeway—limping fast, slower, slow. Even his groan had the creak of an aging shock absorber. Allen Dulles, Director of Central Intelligence, had the gout. (Both brothers suffered such attacks from time to time.) "Where's Foster?" he hissed through teeth tightly clenching a pipe. His face showed the pain, and his words were like edges without a middle.

I stood up behind the desk next to the elevator and replied, "I believe, Mr. Dulles, that Secretary Dulles is in the bathroom."

Allen Dulles pulled the pipe from his mouth, belched, and asked, "What do you do with that, er, sort of . . . thing, that is, my brother's waste products, feces, uh, and such, that is, when he's through, of course . . . ?"

My mind absorbed the Director's question. The Director of the whole Central Intelligence Agency could not be asking me what he was asking me, could he? My reply was halting, but, I think, adequate. "Mr. Dulles, that is a private matter, which, sir, I am not at liberty to discuss, but, you could, of course, raise the matter yourself directly with your brother."

Allen Dulles collapsed into a chair, laughing. "If I did that," he said, "Foster'd think I'd taken leave of my senses, even though he *knows* that the state of his health is of great interest to a number of intelligence services [I was to think back to that remark after the Secretary's death] and that a study of waste products can give indications of health, and so forth, and, oh, well, if I asked him about something like that he'd probably have *you* evict me from this office. Think you could do that—evict me from this office?"

Before I could articulate an answer, he turned to two solemn-faced men who had followed him in, and, after a loud guffaw, he asked them, "What do you two think?"

One of them was big enough to throw *me* out of the

room, looked as though he didn't think much at all, and had the kind of blurred features you always forget. The other one was Kermit (Kim) Roosevelt, grandson of Theodore. *He* was thinking, all right, but not about whether or not I was capable of throwing his chief out of there.

Kim Roosevelt was widely known as an expert in the "destabilization" of governments, and when he told Allen Dulles that "the situation in Egypt is quite different from the one we had in Iran," I listened.

Allen Dulles gave Roosevelt a "that's not what I want to hear!" look, chewed his pipe stem, and studied his gout-ridden foot.

Kim Roosevelt went on. "Nasser is not Mossadegh."

As if in great pain, Allen Dulles grumbled, "Yes, yes, I know that. And Egypt is not Iran. I know that, too."

Before Allen Dulles could say any more, his brother, the Secretary of State, came out of his office, which adjoined his bathroom, and said, "Allen, you look awful."

"The devil's got me," Allen Dulles said petulantly.

"Stalin is dead," his brother replied.

"Foster," Allen said sharply, "if the press hears you calling Stalin the devil, they'll say you're full of religious crap."

"Allen," the Secretary said smugly, "I have been told that, sometimes, in the small hours of the morning, Stalin saw himself as a reincarnation of Satan."

Irritated, the Director of Central Intelligence turned to his two aides, asking, "Why don't *I* know about this?"

"You do, sir," the aide with the forgettable face said.

"I do?" the Director of Central Intelligence responded, incredulously.

"Come into my office!" Secretary Dulles ordered them sternly, using a "Move it or I'll spank you!" tone he got sometimes.

I never really got to *know* Allen Dulles, but we did have

some strange encounters. During one of his fairly regular visits to his brother, for example, I was told to escort the Director to a briefing in another part of the State Department. As we walked down one of the Department's long, antiseptic hallways, he suddenly stopped dead in his tracks, staring at the retreating back of a shapely, and apparently young, woman. Wild-eyed, he turned to me, and shouted, "It's *her!*"

"Who, Mr. Dulles?" I asked.

"Catch her!" he ordered.

"Sir?" I questioned, wondering if he was subject to attacks of something other than gout.

"Hurry! Before it's too late!" he said, shaking.

"I think I know her," I replied, still hesitating.

"*Hurry* you hear, *hurry!*" he yelled, "You *hear?* Hurry."

I went after her. I did know her. A nice young woman who worked on refugee programs (I think that's what she did). When I told her that Allen Dulles wanted to see her, I could feel her fear. "Here?" she whispered.

"Now," I said, softly, pointing back down the corridor to the stricken Director of Central Intelligence.

"How did he find out?" she whispered, her smooth, white face suddenly fatty pudding, rippling and red.

"Find out what?" I asked.

Her eyes drilled me. "You don't *know?*"

I heard the tread of ghosts, scary ghosts, in her voice, but I said, soothingly, "It's okay. Come on."

She looked down the long hallway at Allen Dulles. He was staring back at her. The hallway was still. No one moved. She let out a soft cry, and, then, contempt covering her fatty pudding face, she said, "Lou, you are either playing games with me or you are stupid, and I don't think that you are stupid." With that, hips twitching, she stalked off, away from me and away from Allen Dulles, who was still standing like a statue, staring. I hurried back to him, saying, "She wouldn't talk to you, Mr. Dulles, but I know her."

"Works for Foster, huh?" he grunted in what I thought of as his Dick Tracy tone of voice—sinister with a hidden smile.

"She *does* work for the State Department," I responded, "but I don't think she's even met Secretary Dulles."

"Why do you think she's interested in *you?*" he asked, his voice rising.

"I don't think she is," I replied.

"Don't you play games with me!" he said through pipe-clenching teeth.

Why did they both think *I* was playing a game, I wondered? I said, "I'm married, Mr. Dulles."

"So am I!" he hissed.

Checkmate. Allen Dulles carried, on his face, a sort of rueful serenity and he could be disarmingly straightforward, but I wasn't disarmed. I was alarmed. That same face could be a grille that separated you from him, and, at that moment, the grille was in place. I said, "Mr. Dulles, I repeat, I do not think that she is interested in me, but . . ."

He interrupted with, "She's not interested in *you?*" His eyes were like two venom-filled wounds. He had to struggle to continue. His words crawled all over me as he came up with the startling revelation that "It's Foster she's after!"

"Mr. Dulles, I can't believe that."

I thought his eyes were going to hit me, as he said, "You've got to do your job properly."

"Sir?"

"You must understand," he said, "it's Foster, not you, that she's after. Not me. Not you. Foster! And that's a joke. Hah! She'll find that getting to Foster is like getting to the Rock of Gibraltar. Hah! Mark that. You understand?"

I did not understand, but, in awe of John Foster Dulles' brother and the Director of Central Intelligence, in that order, I assured him that I did understand, and said, "If I can help you in any way . . ."

He thundered his interruption. "*No!* Where's this briefing I'm supposed to be in?"

I pointed, and he left me standing there as he limped down the hall like a panzer attacking in heavy mud. I thought of something his sister, Eleanor, had said to me. "My brother Allen is more human—that means the frailties, too—and, oh, easier to get along with than my brother Foster, but Foster has always been the rock . . . *our* rock. It sounds trite, but, like our Rock of Ages. That's what he's always been—our Rock of Ages."

Allen saw the Secretary as the Rock of Gibraltar, Eleanor as the Rock of Ages. When I passed these two views on to Carl McCardle, Carl, in his usually irreverent fashion, commented, "They both see him as a rock, all right, sure, but they don't see the moss on the blind side of that rock. Maybe they don't want to see it. Maybe they're afraid they'll slip on it. Moss *is* slippery. Did you know that? That moss is slippery?"

"You're saying that Secretary Dulles is slippery?" I asked, with a smile.

"Naw," McCardle replied. "I think he's a rock, too. But, he needs more people around him who know about the moss."

"Know that he's human?"

"Right. Human. Actually, Eleanor does know something about the moss. She understands him pretty well."

She did understand him pretty well. On a flight to Berlin, she told me, "You have the ability to make Foster laugh, Lou. That's valuable. He does have a sense of humor, but, he has problems with it. Guilt . . . something. Probably goes back to our upbringing. Religion. Sense of duty. I don't know. He's always been serious, stern. And, yet, he's always been . . . not so stern, seeing the fun in things, sometimes to a degree that I don't, but, Lou, do keep him laughing, along with everything else that you do."

"In other words, be a gun-totin' court jester," I said lightly.

"'Gun-totin' court jester,'" she repeated, with relish, and continued, "Not many Federal security officers would, in this age of Joe McCarthy, describe themselves *that* way, not to think about laughing about it."

"The Secretary told me that he thought that I was an 'improbable security officer.'"

"You are," she said.

"Yes, ma'am, that's what I am—just a simple ol' security officer."

"Simple like a fox!" she laughed. Then, more seriously, she said, "You are a good security officer, Lou. You wouldn't last long with Foster if you weren't. But, you just seem to have so many things on your mind, so many things seem to interest you—that's what Foster probably means by 'improbable.'"

"Yes," I agreed, "and this job has given me the opportunity to see a great deal, although, in a way, that can be frustrating."

She looked puzzled for a moment. Then she said, "By 'frustrating' do you mean that you see things that you can't do anything about—that feeling of power and powerlessness at the same time?"

"Yes."

She gave a knowing nod. "I know all about *that* sort of thing. But, even so, I've been able to do a lot. I've had a lot of opportunities. But, I've been ready for them, prepared for them. My brother Allen told me that before the Geneva summit conference with the Soviets [in 1955], he told President Eisenhower that, in a way, he felt as if he had been preparing for something like that all of his life, and he had. We, my brothers and I, were always fortunate to have building blocks, opportunities, in our lives. We didn't always have much money—quite the contrary— but we always had the chance to participate, to play a part in great affairs, great events, history. . . ."

"I understand."

"Yes, so, as Allen said, when it came to meeting the Soviets at Geneva, he was ready."

"You mean the intelligence possibilities?" I asked.

"Yes, of course. But, it's deeper than that. The whole confrontation. History. Where we've been. Where we are. Where we're going. Too many people think that one book of Russian history and a subscription to the Sunday *New York Times* qualifies them to negotiate with the Soviets."

"I was at the Geneva summit with the Secretary."

"Yes, I know you were."

"I did a little intelligence work myself, on the side— although I'm not sure that the CIA approves."

"Allen doesn't know?"

"By now, yes."

"My, my, you *are* an 'improbable' security officer."

I never did determine the exact relationship between Allen Dulles and the girl in the hallway, mainly because I didn't want to ask him, and she didn't want to tell me. But that business of Stalin seeing himself as Satan did come up again.

It was another night, another bottle of rye whiskey. We had seen East Berlin. It was bleak. I said so. Secretary Dulles said, "That's what people don't understand. Communism may not be totally evil, but it certainly can be *bleak.*"

I asked him about his use of the phrase "godless Communism."

"It really is godless, now that Stalin is dead," he replied.

"You're not saying that Stalin believed in God, are you?" I asked.

"No. But, I have been told that, sometimes, in the small hours of the morning, he saw himself as the reincarnation of Satan."

"Maybe after too much vodka!" I laughed wonderingly.

"I'm serious," Dulles said, between the click-clucking sounds he sometimes made when he was agitated.

"That's incredible."

"Haven't you seen it in intelligence reports?" he asked. "Remember, Stalin *was* a Georgian."

"Yes, sir, I think I remember hearing you say something like that—about Stalin being Satan—to your brother. And, I did read somewhere that Stalin had a mystical streak, that he was given to some form of hallucination. Things like he regarded Rasputin as a 'positive' force."

"Yes, yes, well, that's probably right, if he actually saw himself as in touch with Satan, or some such."

"Doing the devil's work," I said jokingly, not altogether sure that I was hearing what I was hearing.

Dulles cackled. "All those people who thought that Stalin was the devil incarnate might be surprised to know that he probably agreed with them."

"Why don't you tell them?"

"My Lord, Lou, I've got enough problems already."

"That's true. People'd really think you'd gone off your rocker."

"Indeed."

"But, Mr. Secretary, it would follow, wouldn't it, that if Stalin believed in Satan, he also believed in the reverse."

"You mean God?" Dulles asked, beginning to click-cluck again.

"Yes, sir. And, if he thought that he was Satan, I wonder who he thought was God? You?"

Dulles chuckled. "No. He was so full of suspicions that he undoubtedly saw Satan and God as one."

"So, he was God, too?" I asked, wondering who would ever believe this conversation.

"Something like that," Dulles replied, his words twitching with his face.

"I've heard rumors," I said, "that his top people—Beria, Malenkov, Molotov—murdered him in the end."

"The Black Angels."

"I've never heard them called that.

"Neither have I."

"What do you think, Mr. Secretary?"

"You're the security man, Lou. I'm just the Secretary of State."

4

All that Jazz

There I was in my original, best wash-and-wear suit playing a chorus of "Honeysuckle Rose" with a six-piece combo in a "left-wing" Paris cellar joint when a girl spotted a gun under my jacket and screamed the unmistakable *"Policier! Policier!"*

Somebody yanked the trumpet from my hands while two men grabbed me from behind, and another voice shouted *"Americain!"* and then *"Gingster! Gingster!"*

The police broke through the door and before I could think, at least five of them seemed to have a piece of me. Along with the two already at my back, I was in a crowd. The place was chaos. My shoulders twitched into some form of action, but my reflexes were not good. Much too slow. I had been drinking. My brain cells were wet, but I did know that I did not want them to know who I was because then they would know what I was, and *that* would make the newspapers.

A man with an accent that was not French pulled one of the gendarmes off my shoulder while saying to me, "I will get you out of this. Follow me!" I elbowed him away, and screamed *"God, Country, and one more cigarette!"* thinking that the more noise I made, the less noticeable I would be. Strange faces all around me made strange faces, but the police had unhanded me and were escorting people through the door as the "hoo-haw" sound of more and more police cars filled the air coming in from the streets. A cluster of men who looked like bombed-out used-tomato salesmen staggered past me. Americans? I never found out. Another hand grabbed my shoulder, and, my reflexes improving, I grabbed back, and the man with the odd accent screeched, "Ouch! Easy, easy, I am trying to help." I let him push me toward the door, where I met, coming in, a French detective I knew. He ordered, "Come with me! *Vite! Vite!*" I went, leaving the man with the odd accent behind.

We were speeding away before I asked my friend from the Sûreté how he had known that I was playing trumpet on the Left Bank? He replied, "Your liking for jazz is well known."

"You are having me followed?" I asked, my mouth beginning to feel like I had eaten a bowl of grease.

"It is not necessary," he replied, handing me a flask and adding, "You look terrible."

I took a long pull from the flask, and some of the grease went away while I asked, "Do you know the man who was pushing me out the door?"

"An agent," he hissed, putting his finger to his lips as a sign of secrecy.

"An agent?"

"Mais oui," he replied, "but please do not shout—it is not for the world to know."

This particular detective—from the Algerian section of

the Sûreté—had, over some years, become my friend, or, at least, so I believed. He had, quite literally, taken me home to dinner with his wife and small daughter—a unique opportunity for an American of the time to walk behind the scenes of a middle-class French household. But, as the low-slung Renault swung us out of Saint Germain des Prés, I looked at his profile and wondered if I really did know him. I repeated my question, "How did you know I was playing trumpet over here?"

"History is being written, *mon ami*, and you are one of those on its borders."

Talk about a direct answer, I thought, but said, "Everybody's talking about history's *drainpipe* these days."

I had him. He looked confused. "Drainpipe?"

"Yes. I have not been able to find this drainpipe. Everybody keeps talking about it, and I keep looking for it, but I just can't find it."

"This is most complex," he said, wrinkling his forehead.

"I know."

"'History in a drainpipe'—an unusual concept."

"That it is," I agreed.

"Ah, *oui*, yes. Well, this is Paris and not a drainpipe, and, as I said, your liking of jazz is well known."

"What about that 'agent,' as you called him?"

"He, too, knew of your liking for jazz."

"The whole world seems to know that I like jazz."

He smiled wisely. "It is in your dossier."

I pounced. "Dossier? Where? Here?"

Cheerfully, "Ah, *oui*. Yes. And, elsewhere . . ."

Sarcastically, I said, "To the . . . east . . . no doubt."

Even more cheerfully he answered, "Of course! Exactly. You are of great interest to them. Exactly."

"Great interest?"

"Certainly. Monsieur Dulles—*très formidable*. And you

. . . you are always with him, and that, of course, is of great interest to . . . the east."

"Sometimes," I said, slowly, "I go and listen to folk music, too, around here, in an alley."

"That, too, is known—the American folk singers. *Chansons.* Communists, I think."

"Communists!"

"Yes. You have everybody—what is the expression—'off base'?"

"Who, exactly, does this 'agent,' as you described him, work for? You?"

"*Mais, non!* His employers are, as you said, to . . . the east."

"We *are* talking about the Soviets, here, aren't we?"

"That is possible."

"But is it probable?" I asked, feeling like I was holding the end of a wire without knowing what it was connected to.

"Yes. Definitely probable."

Irritated and confused and still a little drunk, but feeling a terrible kind of exhausted energy, I said, "This information about me undoubtedly has its origins in Siam, or, more precisely, at the court of the King of Thailand in Bangkok."

My detective friend looked at me strangely, but we had pulled up in front of the Hotel Crillon, where I was staying, and he merely asked, "Some coffee?"

"Brandy," I replied, sliding into the street after him.

"Here?" he asked, pointing at the Crillon.

"No," I replied. "Let's walk around to the Ritz. That's where Hemingway drinks. I'll clear my head on the way."

"Ah, Hemingway," my detective friend murmured. "I was once in a fight with him."

We were walking down the Rue Royale, a very civilized street. All the dog droppings seemed to be in the gutter.

My head was beginning to clear just a little. You notice things like that when you are trying to evade the serious questions and you are in Paris thinking about Ernest Hemingway. It crossed my mind that the policeman at my side had the looks of an aging matador, and I had a mental flash of him waving a cape at the embittered bull that was Hemingway of the late fifties. "Who won the fight?" I asked.

"I did, of course," he responded, matter-of-factly.

"How did you manage to beat Ernest Hemingway?" I asked, my voice showing, I'm sure, my wonderment.

As we walked across the Place Vendôme toward the Ritz, he said, even more matter-of-factly, "Because, *mon ami*, I am the police."

There was a damp horse smell in the air, right in the middle of the Place Vendôme, but I did not see any horses. Perhaps the smell was a ghost of old horses. I had heard that in Paris old smells sometimes became ghosts. The "I am the police" had stopped me for a minute. Finally, I said, "But, you actually *hit* him? You actually hit Ernest Hemingway?"

"Only very lightly, at first, when I did not know who he was, and then we, well, restrained him."

"You did not know who Ernest Hemingway *was!*" I exclaimed, feeling shocked and acting very American.

"Only that he was a great drinker, and, as you know, many Americans are great drinkers, and . . . we do not always like such Americans."

We had stopped in front of a banking house I had visited, a place where you never saw money, but always felt its presence. Sort of like being in church. I was beginning to feel depressed. I said, "You do not like Americans who drink, you say, but, *I* drink . . ."

"Yes, *mon ami*, you drink, but, you see, there are drinkers, and, then, there are drinkers—even among Americans—and you we like very much."

I felt touched, but I did not want to admit that I felt touched. I tried to look tough and get back to Ernest Hemingway, as I said, "So, when you found out who he was, you eased off."

"Yes, of course. We regard Hemingway as a friend of France, so . . ."

"So, how did you get in a fight with Ernest Hemingway in the first place?"

We were inside, in the Ritz bar, and the detective was taking a long sip of brandy before answering, while I was trying to get myself suitably awe-struck—the better to "feel" the "spirit" of Hemingway in that hallowed place. Finally, he replied, "Although the Germans had surrendered some years before, Monsieur Hemingway, it seems, had decided that World War II needed one more battle, a battle that started right here and moved, in various stages, around our city."

I was fascinated, and said so, adding, "I wish that I had seen it."

My detective friend nodded, and changed the subject. "You said something most interesting about the Court of the King of Siam [Thailand]."

"The King likes jazz."

"That, too, we have heard."

"Yes."

"Tell me."

So I told him about riding in to Bangkok from the airport, over the quiet, flat countryside, past the storybook houses on stilts, the rice paddies, the Buddhist temples. A lovely ride. Hot. But lovely. Trees, vines, and vegetation of every kind popped up here and there—soft green smears on a dung-colored canvas. And the haze, which changed the light and, in my mind, put the whole scene into an oriental painting that might have been done in Southern France. It was unreal, and unreality came full flower when we arrived at the government guest house—the Pitsanloke House—where we were to stay.

Inside the Pitsanloke House, I was startled by the comforting smell of old newspapers (I thought I was in the library of the old *Washington Post*). I never found the newspapers, but I did find myself lodged in a large suite. It wasn't just large, it was vast, and seemed to be filled with mosquito netting and curling, fleshy plants—dreadful things that looked as though they wanted to wrap themselves around you before they died. It adjoined a shower—a single, lone shower—set into the wall of what appeared to be an empty swimming pool. My security colleague on the trip, Leo Crampsey, took one look and went down into the empty swimming pool and over to the shower which he got under fully clothed and turned on. Having found it necessary to try this myself, although not in such sumptuous surroundings, I left him soaking away.

As I wandered the Pitsanloke's halls, trying to draw a mental map of the place, Bill Macomber rushed up, asking, "Where's the saxophone?"

I was irritated by this interruption to my map-making. "Saxophone? *What* saxophone?"

Macomber's face was eloquent. He gave me his "What planet are *you* from?" look. I backed away from his jutting chin as he snarled, "The Secretary's *gift* for the King."

I found it difficult to take this seriously and said, "I thought we'd packed a brand new 'made in the CIA' type 'Anna' for this King of Siam."

Macomber did not think that that was funny. For that matter, when I thought about it, neither did I. So, I pointed at the cased alto saxophone in the corner, the Secretary's gift for the jazz-loving King, and said, "Don't worry about it—I will personally see that it gets to the palace."

"Should we wrap it?" Macomber asked.

"That's a good-looking case," I said. "Why don't we just leave it as is?"

Macomber rammed his pipe between his teeth, nodded assent, and moved on with ferocious efficiency. I marveled at his ability to keep on top of so many things.

As I watched Macomber leap down some stairs, the Thai protocol chief tapped my shoulder and rose up on his toes bringing his lips almost to the level of my ear, and whispered, "The gift. The gift for the King. The Secretary's gift for the King."

The man was tense. He looked worried, agitated. I tried to be reassuring, saying, "It's right there. Would you like us to wrap it up?"

He studied the saxophone case thoughtfully and said, "No, no. No need to wrap it. It is fine in precisely that condition. But . . . who will take it to the Palace?"

My reply was emphatic. "I will!" I thought that that would be the end of it. But it was only the beginning.

The protocol chief's eyes lit up. He looked me up and down and, suddenly relaxing, murmured, "Ah yes, ah yes. . . . Of course, you will need a black arm band and a black tie."

I knew that the Siamese Court was in mourning over the death of the Queen Grandmother. We had a black arm band and black tie for Dulles. But, I couldn't see any good reason for me to be so attired. I said, "I don't need them. I will take the saxophone along, but I won't actually go into the Secretary's audience with the King and Queen."

"Oh no, no," he responded quickly, adding, "You must, you see." He looked happy as he clapped his hands. A boy standing behind him took off like a rocket, returning in a few moments with a black tie and black arm band. He handed them to me and disappeared again, returning with a large, jewel-encrusted silver goblet. It was more than two feet high and quite beautiful. The protocol chief took it and, with a toothy smile, said, "So now you see, we are entirely ready."

"Fine," I said, wondering just what it was I was getting ready for.

The protocol chief didn't leave me in the dark for long. "You see," he said, plopping the big goblet into my hands, and then placing the cased saxophone on top, "you will carry the gift into his Majesty's presence, thusly, and you will make one step forward from just behind the Secretary, and then you will turn half to the right, at which time Secretary Dulles will take his gift and present it to the King."

I protested. I was not the appropriate person for a mission such as this. "You need," I said, "somebody in knee pants."

"Knee pants?" he questioned.

"Never mind," I said. The man had obviously decided that I was precisely the appropriate person. And his relief at finding a body to execute the one-step-forward and half-to-the-right was so apparent that I did not have the heart to press my protest. Instead, I put on the tie and the arm band, and, with the saxophone under one arm, and the goblet under the other, I went down to the car.

When Dulles came out through the front door, he stopped suddenly by the car, staring sternly at the goblet on the front seat. *"What,"* he asked, "is *that?"*

I scooped up the goblet and horn, and, standing with proper ceremonial dignity in front of the Pitsanloke House, announced, "Mr. Secretary, protocol dictates that I carry your gift of a saxophone to the King like this. Rest assured that I will advise you when it is time for you to present it to his Majesty."

I kept a straight face, but Dulles didn't. At first he seemed to be laughing so hard inside that he couldn't get it outside. When he did get the laugh out, he sounded like a duck in heat, his "honks" and "hoes" shaking, if not scaring, the massed troops and security guards surrounding us. When some words broke through, they sounded something like, "You look marvelous. I hope you put *me* in your memoirs, too." Wonder what he'd think of this.

The protocol chief had assured me that he would be at the palace entrance when we got there and that he would guide us, but I was jumpy and hugged him when I met him standing under the palace portico. He looked frightened, and we had to calm him down. I patted him on the head, and Dulles patted me on the head, and the soldiers around us looked at us as if we were all crazy.

Inside the door, an impressive-looking man, who had taken the protocol chief by the arm, held up a hand for us to stop. The whole procession froze, listening. I listened. It was like listening to a vacuum. Then there was a crash of cymbals and we all moved forward, over heavy carpeting and down gilded hallways into the presence of the twenty-seven-year-old King and his exquisite Queen. The room had a golden simplicity, and they were standing, dressed in western clothes. I made my one-step-forward and half-right.

Dulles' eyes glazed over. He looked dazed, while the King smiled broadly. "Take it, sir," I said to the Secretary, "and give it to the King."

"Can't *you* do it?" Dulles whispered, not moving.

The King's smile got bigger. The Queen looked confused. The protocol chief appeared on the verge of death.

"Mr. Secretary," I said, in a soft shout, "*you* have *got* to make the actual presentation."

"Seems silly, doesn't it," Dulles murmured, still not

moving. I moved the goblet into his stomach. This put the saxophone under his chin. His arms came up, taking it, and thrust it toward the King, his voice booming out, "Your Majesty—for your, uh . . ." He looked back at me, and I whispered "hobby" and he added to the King, "Oh, yes, for your, yes, hobby!"

Later, when I told the King that I had once "sat in" in a "session" with Count Basie's tenor star Lester "Prez" Young, his Majesty bowed.

Outside, the protocol chief bowed to me. Two plainclothes detectives bowed. The uniformed police bowed. The military guards bowed. Aides to the King bowed. Aides to the Queen bowed. Everybody was bowing.

A little later, Dulles commented, "I didn't know you were a musician."

"I'm not," I responded. "I used to play a little jazz, that's all. Oh, I knew and met a lot of fine jazz musicians. Even played with some of them, but, well . . . a good friend of mine, Walter Salb—old Washington music family . . . you probably heard his father play at one function· or another—but, anyway, he once said to me that I had gotten both legs and one arm into the music business, but then I picked up a gun with the free hand and started chasing you."

"What does that mean?" Dulles asked.

"I'm not sure that I know," I said.

"That's a strange name."

"Salb?"

"Yes," he said, "I think I have heard it, and not in connection with music."

"Actually, the family's professions embrace music and the CIA."

Startled, he asked, "The CIA doesn't have a band, does it?"

"I don't think so, although you never know."

"True," he agreed. "I'll have to ask Allen about it."

"Yes, well, some of the family makes music for a living, and some of them, I believe, have worked for the CIA."

He chuckled his words. "A unique combination."

I agreed, adding, "An old friend of *my* family used to make tombstones—'til he went to work for the CIA."

Seriously, Dulles said, "Who knows? Maybe he still makes tombstones."

"I wonder who's under them?"

Dulles said "harumph" and went off with the real boss of Siam—Thailand—Prince Wan, to sign a treaty of cooperation on nuclear matters. When I asked a Thai official where Thailand's "nuclear matters" were located, he pointed to his forehead, and said with great authority, "Here. They are here."

I was reminded of the Pakistani naval officer who had told me that he led a submarine fleet without submarines, but thought better of mentioning it to the Thai official, who apparently carried Thailand's "nuclear matter" behind his forehead, which he kept tapping as he kept saying, "They will come. All things come. To our Ancient Kingdom, all things come, all things come. . . ." He was interrupted by a man who had been identified to me as a Thai intelligence officer who said, "Ah, Mr. Jefferson, you are, we see, an expert of le jazz."

With a smile, I said, "Something for you to put in the file you're building on me, no doubt."

"But of course," he responded. "You are most interesting, and, to us, of course, le jazz is most, most interesting. . . ."

I made a face, I think, but my experience with jazz in Siam, or Thailand (Thailand is, of course, the country's name today, but I guess I just like the sound of Siam better), was not yet over.

That same night, while relaxing with a drink and listening to some jazz records in the spacious and nearly luxurious Bangkok home of a State Department colleague, I slowly, almost imperceptibly at first, began to have a feeling of movement all around me. Actually, many movements, small darting movements, dancing movements, everywhere. I studied the ceilings, the walls, and my eyes gradually absorbed a picture they found difficult to accept—hundreds, perhaps thousands, of fast-moving, lizardlike creatures cavorting around the ceiling and walls like jitterbugging jazz dancers at a senior prom. They were moving in different directions, but in time with the music. They were right on Woody Herman's beat. It was unnerving. I had become accustomed to having hordes of mosquitoes take their naps in my pockets and pants cuffs, and our car had just run over a giant cobra (I thought it was a fire hose) in the driveway, but lizards dancing to the music of Woody Herman! It was too much. I felt a form of overload. My bags weren't packed, but my mind was.

My French detective friend found the cobra more interesting than the lizards, but agreed that the legend of Jefferson and "le jazz" might well have started in Thailand. And he wanted to know more about the sleeping mosquitoes as we talked over the noise of the Ritz bar, which, for the Ritz bar, had gotten quite noisy. "Hordes of sleeping mosquitoes?" he asked in disbelief. *"C'est impossible."*

"I know," I agreed. "It seems crazy. But, what can I say? They definitely needed a lot of rest, which, in a way, is good. The mosquitoes I grew up with in the United States *never* seemed to rest. Of course, in Bangkok, there were so *many* of them, and they all weren't sleeping at the same time. Besides, when they are awake, they are mean, truly mean."

"Mean?"

"Yes. Nasty. Bad. They hurt."

"Ah, *oui* . . . yes, *mon ami*," he said, distracted, adding, "Look over there. Now, there is a man who likes your jazz."

I looked. It was Jean Cocteau. He was wrapped in something that resembled a shroud. His famous nose had the force of a wedge, and his mouth looked as if somebody had bolted it in too tightly. His eyes were sharp and bright. They were coming at me like flame throwers from the side of a knife. I could see the question. It was as if he had a balloon coming out of the side of his head asking, "Where did *you* come from?" Maybe I was imagining it. I didn't think so, but the blaze from his eyes was too much, and I turned away.

Besides my detective and Cocteau, there were only a few serious drinkers left in the bar. It was quiet until an odd, muffled explosion seemed to emanate from the stool Cocteau was sitting on. I looked at my friend, hesitating to comment, for the very good reason that Cocteau had recently been elected to the Académie Francaise, which, officially, made him an "Immortal." If Hemingway was a "friend" of France, then Jean Cocteau must *be* France. However, my companion went right to the point with, "Monsieur Cocteau honors with what you call a . . . fart?"

I laughed out loud. Cocteau's eyes fired their flames right through me as he drained his glass. My detective friend asked, "Would you like to meet him?"

"Do you know him?"

"All France knows Jean Cocteau."

"I'd love to meet him."

We walked over.

My friend introduced us.

I put my hand out.

Cocteau left my hand hanging in air and said something in French too rapid for my comprehension.

"What did he say?" I asked my friend from the French police.

"He said," my friend replied, "that in America man has become a slave to his methods and that he seeks change only for the sake of change."

What did I say to that? Cocteau's eyes held me. I could, quite literally, *feel* the man's intellect. I wanted to say something bright, witty. I tried. "Who was it who said," I asked, "that those obsessed with change should begin by changing for dinner?"

I couldn't tell whether Cocteau understood my question or not, but my French detective was putting it into French, and Cocteau smirked. I think he understood. I added, "I really liked your film *Beauty and the Beast.*"

Cocteau smiled. His stomach rumbled. There was another muffled explosion. My detective friend whispered "Come" and, not too gently, shouldered me away from the "Immortal."

I later told Nelson Rockefeller about being "*there* when Jean Cocteau passed gas in the Ritz."

Rockefeller quaked. Being around Nelson Rockefeller was kind of like being in the middle of a force field, anyway, but the thought of Jean Cocteau farting in the Ritz gave him such a charge that I thought, for a moment, that he was doing an imitation of Elvis Presley without the music. He exclaimed, "If we could just get an *image* of that!"

"A Cocteau original," I volunteered.

"Fabulous!" he cried. "Terrific!" he roared, clapping me hard on the back.

The next time I saw Rockefeller, he immediately asked, "Did you get me that 'Cocteau original'?" This was followed by a modified version of the Elvis Presley dance and the question, "How are ya', fella?"

The business of the "Cocteau original" became a long-running joke between Nelson Rockefeller and me. I can't say that I *knew* Governor Rockefeller, but I saw a lot of him, not only in the fifties, but in the sixties as well, and I liked him. The fact that he was not as "liberal" as the conservatives thought, or quite the "predatory capitalist" seen by many on the left, always fascinated me. As for Rockefeller, the idea of having a joke with Dulles' personal security man seemed to appeal to him, and, as one of the world's great art collectors, I suppose Nelson Rockefeller really would have liked to own that "Cocteau original." In any case, the thought stuck with him. In the early seventies, fifteen years or so after the event, I was visiting in Pennsylvania Senator Hugh Scott's office in the Capitol when Rockefeller came bounding in. I hadn't seen him for at least five years, but I could see the card with my name on it appear behind his eyes, and out of that big grin came, "You never got me that 'Cocteau original'!"

Actually, the night I had my brief encounter with Jean Cocteau, I think that the "Immortal" was drunk or under the influence of some other drug. I later met a man in Spain who claimed to know Cocteau and who told me that one could never be sure whether one was in the presence of the "real" Cocteau or an illusion. He described the French "Immortal" as a "living, breathing, and walking El Greco." As he made that statement, we were seated in El Pardo, former hunting lodge of the kings of Spain and the then residence of General Franco, and we were looking at an El Greco. Dulles was in another room, talking to Franco, and I was talking with an elderly man with a heavily seamed face who said that he was "from the Foreign Office." I had told him about a portrait—not an El Greco—that I had noticed on the way in that reminded me of Jean Cocteau. He got very excited. We waded back through the pile of oriental carpets to the picture, and he stared up at it, murmuring in lisping English, "I never saw it, I never saw it. This will be communicated." He didn't tell me to whom the information was to be communicated, but he introduced me to an old general who, he said, had led the Spanish Blue Division against the Russians during World War II. The old gentleman wore an immaculate uniform, but I had the feeling that his only function now was to occupy space and watch the time pass. He smiled at me and bowed and, in hesitant and lisping English, said that he was pleased to meet me. The man from the Foreign Office gave him a half-salute and turned back to me, saying, "The General does not care for Cocteau, but he does like your American jazz."

The commander of the Spanish Blue Division liked jazz! Somehow, a circle seemed to have been completed.

5

The Ram Dass–John Foster Dulles Connection

During an attempt to fight my way through today's trivia bombardment, I told an old hippie, who has been designated a "San Francisco activist" by the unseen powers, that I was calling a chapter in this book The Ram Dass–John Foster Dulles Connection. As he absorbed this news, the man's already war-torn face took on the appearance of a crushed Styrofoam cup and he pronounced, in no uncertain terms, "Not *even* in San Francisco!"

However, I did come across the following in my journals, journals that I have variously called, I RODE SHOTGUN FOR JOHN FOSTER DULLES, and THE SHADOW OF THE PHANTOM BRINKSMAN:

> John Foster Dulles rose up out of Waikiki's water like a great fish with legs and a tennis hat, and said to the surf, "I do not believe in *little* wars. . . . If I believed in *little* wars, why wouldn't I believe

in *big* wars, and I certainly do not believe in *big* wars. . . .

When I read that, I went searching for a vaguely remembered quote from Ram Dass, "If I'm saving the whale, why am I eating tuna fish?"

That was a strange afternoon on Waikiki beach.

I thought I was used to Dulles, but seeing him like that shook me up.

We were on a "rest and fueling stop" on a trip to Australia (another SEATO conference), and I was standing there in the sand and sun, as Dulles came out of the surf, trying to decide whether to keep my suit coat on, and my gun concealed, despite the heat, or to forget "diplomatic decorum," throw caution to the winds, and cool off. "Decisions!" I whispered to myself, trying to remember what Dulles had just said. He was now standing right in front of me, kicking sand like a bull at the beach. Little wars? I responded (although I don't think he really wanted a response) but, anyway, I responded, "Right! Yes, sir. Absolutely. Little wars can chew you up, like, you remember Carl Sandburg's phrase . . . 'Keep away from the little deaths.' "

Dulles frowned. "Where'd you get *that?*" The inevitable flab on his tough but aging body looked tense. His face still salty-wet, he slipped on the heavy glasses, and the frown eased as he said, "You may have something there." Then he scratched his stomach, a long sweeping scratch, and the frown returned.

I buttoned my jacket.

Dulles growled, "Sandburg was talking about people in taxis that break down. . . ."

"You and Ambassador Dillon . . ."

He cut me off with, "It wasn't Dillon's fault that that taxi broke down, and what I'm saying here is that Sand-

burg was talking about cars that break down, the heat
going off, and such, though . . ."

A woman in an overstuffed bathing suit spotted him
and gave a hyenalike shriek, as I tried to finish his
thought with, "And you are talking about nations and
war."

Dulles was thinking. I was watching the shrieking lady.
One enormous, chocolate-tipped breast had popped out of
her bathing suit. I could see Dulles' mind stop and start
again. He asked, "Is that woman in need of assistance?"

She was being propelled up the beach by two other
women and I replied, "I think she just got a little carried
away."

He squinted and, holding back a smile, said, "She was
probably put there by some sinister group to distract *you*
from your duties."

"We both survived."

"Yes, we did." He chuckled and sat down in the sand.

After a time, he repeated a question I had asked him
before he had gone into the water. "Was it really necessary for us to intervene in Guatemala?"

He looked as though he didn't know the answer. But he
did. "That wasn't a war," he went on, "it was a covert
operation . . . my brother Allen's business . . ." A crooked
smile lit up his face as he covered his feet with sand and
continued, "Of course, we have to be *prepared* to fight
wherever and with whatever is necessary if we are not to
have war—little war, big war, it's all terrible—and, as for
the Soviets and others, their perception of our strength,
and our will to use it, is more important than our actual
strength, and should preclude the necessity for its use,
and if the Soviets or others understand us clearly, they'll
stay out of the little countries, like Guatemala, and we
won't have to take action and end up in a mess, a mess
that kills. Tough stuff, huh?" His eye twitched, and

twitched as he gave a little cackle-cackle-laugh. "The thing is," he continued, "peace is not something you get, now and forever, and then rest. No. It's a process. You have to work at it, day after day, week after week, month after month, year after year." His voice had risen, and he was punching the sand with his fist as he continued, "The thing about a great nation like the United States—for its people—is that it's too easy to assume that its blessings are automatic, when they are not. They are the result of a complex mesh of factors, and . . . a lot of hard work . . . and . . . I'm still wet!"

I handed him a dry towel and some papers, and commented, "Blessings, hard work, pride, and a touch of luck."

He put the papers (one of them was a note from Eisenhower) under a rock in the sand and said, "Sometimes you have to make your own luck, and, pride, yes, but in what you do rather than what you get. . . ."

A battered truck shook its way down the beach behind us, its engine sounding like an earthquake in a junkyard. Dulles looked back at it, and snorted. "Part of our civilizing influence on these islands."

My eyes were on an absolutely gorgeous Eurasian woman who handed me a bottle of macadamia nuts and strolled off. I said to Dulles, "That was very nice of her."

He grabbed the nuts out of my hand and smirked. "Is all this pulchritude for your benefit or mine?"

"God blesses those who bless themselves," I replied.

"An unusual way of looking at it," he said, picking up a handful of sand and letting it slide slowly between his fingers. He threw some at me, and I ducked and thought my gun was sliding from its holster under my jacket. I grabbed for it, and he said, "Don't shoot!"

"I thought I was going to drop it," I said.

He laughed. "Did you know that some people see the future in the sand?"

"I hope nobody hears you talking like that."

He had a coughing spasm. When he got it under control, he said, "I think some of the Congress tries to make foreign policy out of sand, but I don't have that privilege."

"As I said—God blesses those who bless themselves."

Dulles' shoulders shook. "That's good!" he said, "although there are times when I am forced to wonder . . ." (Contrary to popular opinion, Dulles did not believe that he had a private wire to the Almighty.)

"You wonder?" I questioned.

"Actually," Dulles continued, sifting sand, and picking up where he'd left off some minutes before, "we must beware of small wars in small countries for limited reasons—Korea should never have happened—because, aside from any morality involved, they can get out of hand, you can lose control, events can govern you, rather than you governing events. But, they won't happen in the first place if your opponents believe that you won't allow them to happen, that we will come down hard if we have to, that we practice what Herman Phleger [Dulles' legal adviser] calls 'lumber camp law'—you put the pencil and the gun on the table at the same time. Sounds tough, huh? Sometimes you *have* to stand tough to keep the peace . . . to keep people from whittling away at it. I don't believe in just a little *bit* of peace. I believe in peace. You can't have it both ways. And you've got to be prepared to fight if you want peace. That's the irony. But you can't have peace if you announce you *won't* fight. They'll come right after you or one of your friends. Look at Korea. Yes, for a nation like the United States—the target of envy and greed, unjustified and justified—to have peace in this imperfect world, it must have power. It's just crazy, sometimes. I mean I often see the very Americans who want to tell the rest of the world how to function, how to hold elections, who's Right and who's Left, who they should put in charge and who they should throw out, yes, tell them all that and heaven knows what else, and then, at the same time, want this country to give up its power."

"Many Americans feel guilty over America's power," I said, "and refuse to realize that it is because of that power that we are in a position to do good."

Dulles nodded and shook all over as he burrowed his posterior into the sand while precariously hanging on to a paper cup full of rye whiskey with one hand and holding too many macadamia nuts with the other. Some of the whiskey spilled on the portion of the note from Eisenhower not covered by the rock. "Did I read that letter from the President?" he asked.

"I think you did, Mr. Secretary."

"Yes, I think I did," he agreed sourly.

"You know," he said suddenly, "I can never fathom those who seem to believe that America is always and automatically wrong, and yet, at the same time, view good plumbing as an inalienable right."

Taking it as a joke, I said, "Some of my best friends are like that."

"Well," he said, seriously, "if they keep it up, then, at best, the standard of living they take for granted will be gone, and, at worst, well, if the Soviets ever see that the 'balance of forces' has turned strongly in their favor, then I'm afraid America will suffer a lesson in foreign policy from which she may not recover—indeed, from which the world may not recover."

"But, Mr. Secretary, the United States is much stronger than the Soviet Union."

"For the moment, yes. I hope that will continue. But, change is a law of life—things are always changing—which means that you have to take the situation as it is *each day*, day after day. That's what diplomacy is all about—not one big, grand scheme, but keeping the peace one day at a time, day after day after day. You can't understand the past, or write the future, without acting in the present." He laughed, adding, "But, that's too simple for most people." His laugh got larger. "It's amazing, but with many people, the more complications there are, the larger the reality. No, you just have to take it *each day*."

It's odd, but those words did not really come into focus for me until just a few years back when I saw a sign outside Armadillo World Headquarters in Austin, Texas—Willie Nelson was featured at the time—but the sign said, WE MUST SEE INTO THE PRESENT—IT IS BETWEEN THE PAST AND THE FUTURE.

Dulles had a sense of position.

He understood where he was.

I doubt that I will ever forget the overbearing reporter who, on that stop in Hawaii, popped up before us on the beach and asked Dulles if he spoke "with the authority of the President."

Dulles replied, acid etching every word, "I do not speak with the President's authority—of course not—but I can assure you that when I speak, I speak with authority."

The reporter scratched his head.

"Why are you scratching your head?" Dulles asked.

The reporter scratched his head again. His face reflected a feeling of superiority, arrogance. He was the kind of guy who would wear a sweater around his neck. He didn't have a sweater around his neck, but you knew he was capable of it. He smirked as he said, "I think I have a flea."

"Ahhhhhh, a flea," Dulles murmured. "Now I understand the thrust of your question."

Taken aback, the reporter asked, "What do you mean?"

A small smile creased Dulles' face. "You wish me to speak with authority on fleas?" he asked.

"Of course not," the reporter snipped, trying to look dangerous, but failing.

"Fleas," Dulles repeated, looking straight at him.

The reporter was obviously regretting having brought up the whole subject as he tried to turn the conversation, "It's being said that you live in the past."

Dulles grunted, and growled, "I *study* the past so that we will *have* a present—so that we won't make the same mistakes, mistakes that might have been fatal for a few then, but that today could envelope untold millions. And . . ."

The reporter tried to interrupt him. "That's all . . ."

Dulles waved him down with, "*And*, if we lose the present, the future is difficult to contemplate."

"You *do* speak with authority," the reporter said, quietly.

"Yes, I do," Dulles said, "and you would do well to listen while we both still have the freedom for an exchange such as this." As he spoke, his tone took on that special Anglo-Saxon blend of self-righteous self-interest that he professed (sincerely, I think) to disdain in such British Establishment figures as Anthony Eden.

The reporter snarled. Blood appeared ready to burst right through his forehead. I almost wished the poor guy had a sweater around his neck to give him confidence. But the confrontation was suddenly swarmed over by Japanese tourists hitting the beach in business suits. Dulles, forgetting the reporter, said, "When I was drafting the Japanese Peace Treaty, people told me that I should draft a treaty that would 'keep the Japanese down'—hah!"

At that point, a man with a crazed look sidled up to me,

whispering, "Is this a secret meeting?" I took off my suit jacket. The man left abruptly when he saw the gun.

The reporter left, too.

The lady with the macadamia nuts reappeared, looked over at me, and dropped her nuts.

A bronzed beachboy pointed at me, shouting, and the Japanese all looked back and tripped over each other.

Dulles slapped my back, and said, "Everybody's looking at your gun."

"No real harm in that," I responded, feeling embarrassed. I knelt in the sand, got some clean paper cups, and poured us both some Old Overholt. Drinking seemed like a good idea. I was not a morning drinker at the time, but I surely was an afternoon drinker, and it was the heart of the afternoon. Dulles was not an afternoon drinker. I think that he could have become one if he had thought about it on enough afternoons, but, I suppose, he never had the time. In any case, we proceeded to drink the heart right out of that particular afternoon, with Dulles rumbling—his voice down in deep bullfrog—things like, "Roles are imposed on individuals and nations alike." His eyes would close and open and close and open.

"My God!" I interrupted during one closed-eye period. "That woman with the loose breast is coming back."

Opening one eye, he looked. "I'm asleep," he said and closed the eye and dozed. Small snores put commas to the wave-crash as the woman with the unhampered breast kicked up sand in front of us. As I watched the oddly sexless lady jump up and down, my thoughts rattled back to Indonesia the week before, when it had appeared that a woman was tossing a bomb at our car, and I had forced Dulles, who was thirty pounds heavier than I, to the car floor. It was not a bomb. It was a balled-up leaflet, which I still have. But it had certainly looked like a bomb as it came at us out of a crowd that was shouting "Go home

Dulles!" There weren't as many combat zones in those days as we seem to have now, but there were some. Dulles said later, "Lou, if that *had* been a bomb, I guess we would have died in each other's arms."

"That would have been historic," I replied.

He twinkled, and barked, "It is more blessed to be alive than to be historic."

I couldn't resist, "Better red than dead?"

That set him off. "No! Good Lord!" I could see him warming up. Here we go again, I thought. "Americans," he barked, "take the benefits of the American system—capitalism, free enterprise, whatever you want to call it—for granted, as if they were automatic, but when they don't get their candy, well . . . that's enough of *that!*"

"People can't have it both ways."

"No, and I've got to keep my sense of humor."

"Lot of people don't think you *have* a sense of humor."

"I know," he said thoughtfully, "I do take life pretty seriously, but . . ."

I completed his sentence. "You *have* a sense of humor."

"I do have a sense of humor, and," he said decisively, "I have *got* to keep it."

Keeping his sense of humor wasn't that much of a problem for Dulles. Just prior to the swim off Waikiki and the bomb that wasn't a bomb in Indonesia, we spent a week at a SEATO conference in Karachi, Pakistan, where Dulles tried to steam open and reseal the wrapping paper around his gift for a high Pakistani official. Fearful that he would destroy the paper, he asked my security colleague, Leo Crampsey, for assistance. He told Leo that he just wanted to "have another look." Leo took care of it, and Dulles was so impressed that he spread the word that Leo was "good with packages." Soon, everyone was asking Leo to *wrap* packages. Leo was infuriated, grumbling to me, "I'm no damn gift wrapper! I'm a Security Officer for the United States Department of State!"

It took a day or so, but he got over it. I thought packages were forgotten until just before our departure, when Dulles came rushing out of the Embassy residence library shouting at Bill Macomber, "I thought I told you to have that set of George Washington's writings delivered to the Governor-General!"

Macomber, puzzled, said, "Mr. Secretary, they were delivered yesterday."

"*Yesterday!*" Dulles unloaded the word like a cannonball. Then he pointed into the library and, his voice dropping, added, "Well, then, what are they doing on that table in there?"

Sure enough, there they were, piled neatly on a handsome old table. The Complete Works of George Washington. We all stared. Then Dulles asked, "*Where* are my detective stories? The paperbacked ones. They were wrapped in tissue paper."

Macomber's words were almost inaudible. "Leo must have made a mistake."

"Leo?" Dulles questioned. "What does Leo have to do with *this?*"

I was afraid that Macomber would bite his pipe stem in two. He pulled it from between grinding teeth just in time and told the Secretary, "You gave Leo such a reputation as a package wrapper that, yes, Mr. Secretary, I did ask him to wrap the books for the Governor-General, and . . ."

Dulles looked like that bird that has just learned that instead of being an eagle, it is a crow. He said softly, "That may be, but he wrapped the wrong books and the Governor-General of Pakistan must now have my paperbacked detective stories as a State gift from the rich and powerful United States of America."

The room was silent for a moment, all of us, I am sure,

contemplating the significance of this switch from George Washington to Agatha Christie on the chessboard of world affairs. Then, looking more like the crow who has just found out that, after all, it is actually an eagle, Dulles roared with laughter, saying, "Why, that's marvelous. Absolutely marvelous."

Macomber did not look as though it was marvelous. I wondered if Leo had plane fare home. But Dulles cracked up. He became nearly incoherent, mumbling something about some countries being leatherbacked and other countries being paperbacked. Leo appeared. He was immediately surrounded by Dulles and Macomber, and I thought that he was going to bolt until he realized that it was all very friendly. After a minute, the three of them, in a festive mood, headed in to wrap for delivery the Complete Works of George Washington. I was standing off in a corner with the Pakistani naval officer who had informed me that although Pakistan had no submarines, *he* had been appointed chief of the Pakistani "Submarine Force." He said that his appointment had been made in the hope that he would be able to nudge the United States into giving Pakistan submarines, thus allowing it to "fulfill its mighty destiny under the seas." As he stood next to me, absorbing the situation of the books, he whispered in my ear, "Could this mean that, perhaps, now, we will get our submarines?"

"Instead of the Complete Works of George Washington?" I whispered back.

"No," he responded. "In *exchange* for Mr. Dulles' favorite detective stories."

"But, we are going to deliver the Complete Works of George Washington!" I exclaimed.

"That I can see," he said. "But, *we* still have the detective stories."

"You mean that you are going to hold Secretary Dulles' favorite paperbacked detective stories *hostage?*" I asked.

"That," he said, his face somber, "is a distinct possibility."

"My God."

He smiled. "You and I, my friend, pray to different gods, although they are, perhaps, cousins."

Thoughts of the Deity and my conversation with the chief of the phantom submarine fleet ceased suddenly when I remembered the detective story from the Secretary's collection that I had been reading on the aircraft and the pornographic postcard from Paris that I had been using as a bookmark. Was it still there? In the book? At the Governor-General's? I couldn't remember. But that night, at the State dinner, after Dulles apologized to the Governor-General for the mix-up of the books, the Pakistani leader said that in a way he was disappointed because "the detective stories . . . and . . . er . . . everything . . . were so . . . unexpected," whereas the Complete Works of George Washington were the sort of thing one usually got.

The detective stories were returned, including the one that had held the pornographic postcard, but without the pornographic postcard. When they met after that, I noticed that there was a small leer in the Governor-General's eyes when he looked at Dulles. I asked my naval friend if he knew what the Governor-General had meant by "and . . . er . . . everything . . ." but all he would say was, "We *deserve* the submarines!"

However, the highlight of that week in Karachi was not the affair of the books, but a Torch Light Tatoo held in honor of the principal delegates to the conference, and the Shah of Iran, who, coincidentally, was making a state visit to Pakistan. I had first learned that the Shah was in town from a Pakistani detective who had had three special women brought in from somewhere near Nepal to entertain his Imperial Majesty. I didn't see the Persian potentate, though, until the night of the Tatoo, when he hurtled in through the heat and humidity with so many cars and outriders that we couldn't find a place to put Dulles' limousine. I got mad. When told that Dulles was only a Foreign Minister, whereas the Shah was an Emperor, and that we would therefore have to park almost a mile away, I announced to everyone within earshot that if we did not get one of the many parking places occupied by the cars in the Shah's party, I would abolish the Shah. A booted and spurred Iranian officer asked, in disbelief, "Is that a threat?"

"No!" I replied, angrily. "It is a fact. But, don't worry, I won't hurt him. I'll just abolish his job. That is the civilized way."

The whole thing got crazy. An Iranian bodyguard pointed a rifle at me. A Pakistani policeman grabbed the rifle, pushing its barrel skyward before it went off. One of the uniformed Iranian aides pulled his saber and started flailing around like a Cossack gone berserk. Luckily no one was hurt, but, for a few minutes, it seemed as if we were on the brink of a riot, if not a war. In the end, they were all so dumbfounded by my apparent fearlessness that we got a decent parking space.

During my parking-space confrontation with the Iranians, a Karachi police inspector and my friend from the "Submarine Force" watched the Dulleses. When I finally got back to them, I noticed Mrs. Dulles beckoning to me from one of four thronelike chairs. The other three were empty, but were being held for the Secretary, the Shah, and his then current Empress, Saroya, who had become a "problem of State" for the Shah because she apparently could not conceive a child. To keep the Shah happy, the CIA had reportedly hired a gynecologist to help her out.

When the CIA gynecologist failed in his mission, the Shah's resentment of the CIA's role in his taking and holding power turned into contempt. If they could not help him produce an heir to the Peacock Throne, then what good, really, were they? Anyway, I worked my way through the cluster of military and security aides to Mrs. Dulles' side. She asked me to sit down on the Secretary's throne, which was next to the Shah's throne, which was next to Saroya's throne (the Shah and Saroya were just being seated) and watch the show with her. Dulles was a few seats down, in deep conversation with the British Foreign Secretary. Janet Dulles said to me, "Lou, sit down. I know how much you like bagpipes, and Foster is quite occupied down there with the other Foreign Ministers." I looked down at the Secretary, assuring myself that the police had him well covered, and sank down into the throne as the bagpipes sounded in the distance.

I eyed the Shah, to my left, covertly, out of the corner of my eye. He was in a uniform even more resplendant than those of the many military aides surrounding him. I told Mrs. Dulles that I now understood why the Iranian throne was called the Peacock Throne. She was in good spirits, not noticing, or perhaps ignoring, the contempt with which the Shah and his glamorous aides were eyeing my wash-and-wear suit and fuzzy face (I looked as though I had shaved with a dull rock). One of the Shah's men kept sticking his head between her head and mine as he darted, jumped, and leaped around behind us. He reminded me of a dancing rat. He made me nervous, and, worse, he made Janet Dulles nervous. I finally told him to sit down, and the Shah turned to me and asked, his voice low, his words walking on stilts, "Who, *really*, are you?"

What did I say to that? He damn well knew *what* I was. I almost didn't answer at all. Then, inspiration blessed me. I remembered a call girl named Thelma "Ping" Pong, who, I knew, had spent more than a couple of nights with him in New York. So I replied, "Your Majesty, I am a friend of Thelma Pong—you *do* remember '*Ping*' Pong, do you not?"

His eyes glittered. I heard him say, "Do not trifle with me. . . ." before the arrival of the bagpipes in front of us drowned out our conversation.

But, back to the beach at Waikiki where Dulles and I were ducking Japanese tourists and hiding important papers under rocks. He recalled the parking space confrontation, which he called my "small war with Iran," and said that he hoped that I had learned something from it.

I told him, tongue in cheek, that I believed that I had "avoided war because they knew I was ready to fight."

"Your intentions were clear." He chuckled.

"They were definitely clear," I said, feeling the anger of that night in Karachi come back to me. "I was so angry I was prepared to back them up, too."

"What did you tell them you would do?" he asked.

"Abolish the Shah's job."

"Did you really say '*abolish* the Shah's *job*'?"

"Well . . ."

"That's all right," he interrupted, looking quite happy with the whole idea, "although I would have to say that I am grateful that you did not find it necessary to come to me and tell me that we had to abolish the Shah's job."

"Sir, I . . ."

"I'm sure that nobody else ever threatened to abolish the Shah's job. Murder him, maybe. But, abolish his *job*? No. *That* is an accomplishment."

"We got the parking space."

"Did we really *need* that parking space?"

"Yes."

"Good."

My tongue was almost, but not quite, out of my cheek. "Actually, Mr. Secretary, I kept the peace, didn't I?"

"You did, indeed." He laughed. "And we do have to keep the peace at every level."

"We must be consistent," I said, trying to work my tongue completely out of my cheek.

"Yes. And, the more I think about it, your willingness to fight for a parking space had considerable significance."

"I'm glad you see it that way. Some of the Europeans describe the United States as one big parking lot."

"Jealousy," Dulles said, decisively.

"Yes, sir," I agreed, "but, thinking of *your* philosophy, if we won't fight for one small parking space, people will wonder if we'll fight for the big one."

His eyebrows closed in on each other. "The important thing is, because of your clarity of purpose, you did not have to fight at all. Your intentions were just, and, although you did not wish to fight, you were prepared to fight, and they knew it. Above all, perhaps, you were consistent with your own image."

"I was?"

"Yes. And, consistency is crucial."

Consistency is crucial. Or, if I'm saving the whale, why *am* I eating tuna fish?

6

At the Summit

We were in Paris, on our way to Geneva for the first post–World War II summit meeting with the Soviets, when, in an elevator in the Hotel Crillon, Dulles collided with Charlie Chaplin, who stuck his tongue out, fell to his knees, and shot back up while making a closed-mouth sound—"Shooooosh-a-Whoooosh-a-SHOOOSH-a-Whoooshashoooshashoosh . . ."

Dulles merely said "Harumph" as two Arab women got on the elevator behind us.

I thought Chaplin was going to take a bite out of Dulles' shoulder, but, instead, he continued the strange, closed-mouth "ShooooooooshaWhoooshAshoooshawhooooooosh" sound. The two Arab women looked furtively around the elevator, trying to find the origin of the odd noise, obviously not recognizing either Dulles or Chaplin.

I said, "Hello, Mr. Chaplin," and the famous comedian's motionless face gave out with a new sound—"chit, chit, chit"—while Dulles belched up another "Harumph" and the two Arab women looked terrified as the elevator doors opened and Chaplin touched hips with one of them. Then, looking suddenly dignified and lordly, Charlie Chaplin departed from the elevator. The two women held back until the comedian was well away from the door and then leaped through, shrieking.

As the elevator continued its journey, Dulles said, "I think that Charlie Chaplin has achieved another dimension."

"I thought he was going to take a bite out of your shoulder," I responded, as we left the elevator for a "secret" meeting, and were met by reporters, one of whom asked, "Mr. Secretary, is it true that you are meeting secretly with Mr. Charles Chaplin?"

"We have had our meeting," Dulles replied with a straight face.

"Where?" the reporter asked, looking up and down the hall.

"On the elevator," Dulles said.

The reporter was persistent. "What did you discuss?"

Dulles looked at me, and I volunteered, "After Mr. Chaplin did not take a bite out of Secretary Dulles' shoulder, they discussed Arab women."

"Yes." Dulles laughed. "Arab women!" He strode off down the hall to his "secret" meeting, his stunned questioners staring after him.

We had left Washington for Paris and Geneva on the afternoon of July 13, 1955, in Harry Truman's old *Constellation*. It was a seventeen-hour flight in those prejet days—time for a lot of talk. State Department Legal Adviser and San Francisco lawyer Herman Phleger started right in with a riddle about a brick—i.e., if one brick weighed "q" and you put "y" and "z" and "q" together, and, well, it went on and on, and I don't think anybody ever got the answer, or, for that matter, the question. Phleger was unusual. A man who had known Dulles on Wall Street commented, "Phleger's *got* to crack. I mean, how can *any*body be John Foster Dulles' lawyer?" A good question. But, Phleger managed. Dulles liked what he called "Herman's lumber camp approach" to the law. Indeed, on the plane, he asked Phleger if he'd heard "this brick story in a lumber camp?"

Phleger said, "No, but I *told* it in some lumber camps."

"A delaying tactic?" Dulles asked.

"A good one!" Phleger replied.

Assistant Secretary of State for Europe, Livingston Merchant, a key adviser and urbane gentleman, joined in with, "I myself have not had much occasion to think upon bricks, except, of course, old bricks in colonial houses."

Dulles, chewing salted peanuts, crunched his question, "Is there a point to this, Herman?"

Phleger assured him that there was and started a discourse on how one weighed a brick, at which point Carl McCardle remarked, "Wonder what the Russians are talking about on *their* plane heading for this 'big meet' with us? They sure as hell aren't talking about *bricks!*"

"How do you know that, Carl?" Livingston Merchant asked.

"Carl's right," Dulles said.

The brick got misplaced.

Sleeping accommodations on that flight were, for me, memorable. Merchant wrote in a little memoir, *Recollections of the Summit Conference:* "We had eleven aboard this trip. Since the plane sleeps only ten passengers, the security man, Lou Jefferson, being young and vigorous, was presumed not to mind sleeping on the floor."

Actually, I slept in a baggage rack.

Our stop in Paris was brief, and we came down over Geneva just one half hour before the arrival of President Eisenhower. Switzerland from the air was lovely—large mountains, little houses, and lots of train tracks. Somebody has described Switzerland as a "great, big beautiful train set." I was entranced until, after landing, I had a fully cocked "burp" gun jammed into my chest by a scowling Swiss soldier, who looked as though he might floss his teeth with barbed wire. All my life I had heard Switzerland described as a neutral country, but at that moment I could only think, "This man does *not* look neutral!"

Eisenhower was coming down the steps they had run up the side of his gleaming aircraft, and I ducked under the "burp" gun, hoping the soldier wouldn't shoot me. Happily, he didn't. Instead, he swung his gun toward Dulles. I grabbed the muzzle in my fist, wondering if I'd lose my fist. The soldier's eyes, startled, bored into mine, but he didn't pull the trigger, and, when an officer started shouting at him, he eased back. Dulles said, "Lou, we are not at war with Switzerland!" and headed toward Eisenhower, running right into the barrel of another Swiss "burp" gun. Two Swiss-German officers started shouting *"NEIN, NEIN, NEIN!"* The gun barrel nudging Dulles' chest moved away, but others swung toward us. It was close. Too close. I shouted, "STOP IT!" so loudly that Eisenhower looked over, and the Swiss Army parted as if, in the words of a Secret Service agent, "they thought Eisenhower was Moses and our Cadillacs were the sea."

Dulles climbed into one of the Cadillacs with Eisenhower. I jumped into the Secret Service follow-up car, relieved to get out of there alive.

The Secretary and Mrs. Dulles were quartered in a villa above Lake Geneva. Shortly after our arrival, the Russians in the person of Soviet Foreign Minister Molotov (and entourage) pulled in with screaming brakes and a great gravel skid. Molotov's security force was led by a big, swarthy KGB "Colonel" who looked as if he had been put together by an armorer. Over a chunky frame he wore a white tunic with gold shoulder boards, light blue trousers, and a dress-white cap. Very fancy. But, beside him was a security man dressed in a suit that looked as if it had been cut in a darkened room with a chain saw. The man's neck was an extension of his shoulders, and he had a steel tooth right in the center of his smile. Scary.

Molotov, with his pince-nez spectacles and deceptively mild manner, gave three grunts and a hand touch to Dulles and went into the villa, leaving his garish "Colonel" outside staring intently at me. A Swiss detective who spoke both Russian and English made the introductions— "Colonel Alexandrov, Monsieur Jefferson. Monsieur Jefferson, Colonel Alexandrov."

Alexandrov nodded, slowly. The man in the chain-saw suit pushed his mighty stomach into my side. He was enormous. The sheer volume of his flesh was staggering. One of the Swiss detectives pulled me away from him and whispered in my ear, "The Russian—he is homosexual."

"In the uniform?" I whispered back.

"No, no. The fat one. The Colonel? We do not know. But his colleague, a peasant, yes, but notorious!"

Alexandrov had come over to us, leaving his massive companion behind. I put out my hand. Alexandrov looked down at it like it might be a bomb. Finally, after what seemed like a full minute, the KGB Colonel's hand crept out. It was big and limp—a mighty force immobilized. Our hands touched. That was it until, seemingly out of nowhere, a Russian cigarette appeared in that big, limp hand. He thrust it toward me. I took it and offered him an American cigarette, which he in turn took. I then aimed my pack of cigarettes at the massive man in the chain-saw suit, who, instead of taking a cigarette, very deliberately spit on the ground. That closed the ceremonies. Shortly thereafter, Molotov came out. He looked even grimmer than his colonel. You could almost see the violence gnawing away at his belly. But he was controlled. Terribly controlled. They left. Dulles waved as they kicked up more gravel, but Molotov did not look back. I remarked that "Molotov doesn't seem very happy."

Dulles nodded and said, "Molotov's definition of 'happy' and your definition of 'happy' would not be the same."

Following this preliminary skirmish with Molotov, Dulles picked up the phone and got hold of then British Foreign Secretary Harold Macmillan and said, "Harold, let's go swimming." Within minutes we were at a narrow beach flanked by Lake Geneva on one side and Dwight Eisenhower's villa on the other. Macmillan was right behind us, chirping away. "I say, Foster, did Ike say it was all right for us to swim here?"

"You know Ike," Dulles chuckled, taking off the robe that covered his swimming shorts. "What he doesn't know . . . and so forth . . ."

"Yes, yes, of course," Macmillan acknowledged, and, after unbuttoning an old sweater that he seemed to share with a group of invisible moths and aiming himself toward a beach chair, which he nearly missed (his moves were often reminiscent of an old newspaper being blown about by a strong wind), he added, "Well, Foster, that's all the clothes *I'm* taking off, anyway. . . . Old wounds, and all that, you know—guardsman business, and so forth, but, Foster, eruppp, uh, you swim and all that, and, then, we, uh, can have a little, uh, chat . . . what?"

With Macmillan, whose manner of speaking has been described as "burble-speak," comfortably sprawled in a beach chair, sipping Scotch, Dulles entered the icy water. Fully dressed, but right behind him, I tested the water with one finger and shivered. The Swiss police had a boat just off shore. "Burp" guns were everywhere. So, feeling secure, I sat down beside Macmillan, who said, "That, uh, water, it's quite, er, cold, uh, that is, isn't it?"

"It is, indeed!" I replied.

Macmillan smacked his lips. Then, "Do you, erumph, uh, think this . . . this . . . immersion in ice . . . is, er, part of Foster's preparation for his next meeting with Molotov?"

"I think," I replied, "that he *does* 'train' for his bouts with Molotov, but not by swimming in ice water. No, he does that for fun."

Macmillan's face had many creases and small bulges, all of which were moving as he pursued the subject. "For fun, yes. Of course. Erruppppp. Quite. But, you say that he does *'train'* . . . for these, er . . . 'bouts' . . . with Molotov?"

"Well, now, sir," I said, "I don't mean that he eats raw meat . . ."

"I have *seen* him eat raw meat!" Macmillan responded, clearly, his fingers fluffing at his moustache.

"Before Molotov?" I asked.

"No, before caviar," Macmillan replied with a chuckle.

I came back with, "Secretary Dulles did ask me once if I knew anything about Joe Louis' training methods?"

"Joe Louis!" Macmillan exclaimed. "The *prize*fighter?"

"Yes."

"My God," Macmillan said, his crunchy face taking on the look of a doctor announcing a patient's demise. "Poor Molotov," he concluded softly.

Was he serious, I wondered? I said, "Secretary Dulles has already seen Molotov."

Macmillan squinted. It was a deep squint. The corners of his eyes were pleated. "Quite," he murmured. "Yes. Quite. Indeed. Perhaps he's merely cleansing himself out there in that awful water, what?"

Macmillan was amazing. He was not simply an aristocrat. He was more like an oil painting. An *old* oil painting with the cracks lacquered over. I found him fascinating, and I liked him, but before I could formulate a suitable reply to this latest observation, Dulles came up out of Lake Geneva snorting and bellowing, saying, "Best thing in the world, Harold. Best thing in the world. Keeps you fit. Ready for anything."

"*Any*thing, Foster?" Macmillan asked.

"Indeed, yes, Harold," Dulles replied.

Macmillan rattled his throat and lisped, "Quite, Foster, quite. A blessing. Yes, indeed, a blessing."

"Clears the brain," Dulles continued, shaking his head and shoulders, showering water in all directions. He was obviously invigorated, his tone razor-sharp, as he added, "Excellent before a negotiation, Harold."

Macmillan arched an eyebrow and muttered through his whiskers, "Yes, yes, quite. That's what I was tellin' y'r man here." His words slurred into each other as he added, "Or was *he* tellin' me? One way or another, we were discussin' it. . . ."

Dulles pulled on his robe and gave me a hard stare. "What was Harold telling you, Lou?" he asked.

"Something about swimming in cold water being good preparation for dealing with Molotov, Mr. Secretary."

Dulles studied Macmillan suspiciously. "Yes, yes. I see."

Macmillan gurgled some words. "You did look rather like a whale, Foster."

"What's that to do with Molotov?" Dulles asked, looking irritated. Then, his face clearing, he asked, "How do whales match up with sharks, Harold? Molotov's certainly a shark, wouldn't you say?"

Before Macmillan could get off an answer, a Swiss detective came running up, shouting, "The boat! The police boat! They want to know if that was President Eisenhower swimming?"

The detective had been at the airport, and, I thought, certainly knew the difference between Eisenhower and Dulles. I said, "*Mon ami,* you *know* that *that* is John Foster Dulles, don't you?"

"Of course," the detective replied matter-of-factly, "but I

thought that perhaps you might wish them to *think* that it was Eisenhower." His English was perfect.

"Why would I want to do that?" I asked.

"That is for *you* to determine."

I was puzzled. "You're giving me options?"

His smile was polite. "Options? Yes, of course. Options. You see, sometimes it is best that things not appear to be what they are."

"Sounds like the Russians."

His smile was broad. "Ah, yes. You are correct. It is very Russian."

"Russian-type thinking," I said, adding, "Swiss, too, maybe?"

His smile got broader. "Perhaps."

"You are most considerate," I said.

The detective pointed skyward, saying, "Look!"

I looked up and saw what appeared to be a flying saucer coming down out of the Alps. "What is it?" I asked, as it stopped its descent and started a near vertical ascent, rapidly disappearing into the atmosphere.

The detective merely smiled a little more. Dulles called, "Did you see that?"

"Yes, sir," I called back. "Looked like a flying saucer."

"No, no," the Swiss detective grunted.

"Ike believes in those things," Dulles said to Macmillan.

Macmillan muttered a few incomprehensible words before asking, "You are, er, uh, saying Ike believes in, uh, flying *sau*cers?"

"He does," Dulles replied, looking skyward. "I wonder if he saw that one?"

"Lunacy!" Macmillan muttered. Actually, it was more of a "snutter" than a mutter—a Macmillan aide had told me that "the Foreign Secretary does not snicker, nor does he mutter. He *snutters*."

"What do you *mean*, 'lunacy'?" Dulles asked, looking angry.

Macmillan seemed to be working his nose down into his moustache as, petulantly, he said, "Nothing, Foster. Nothing at all."

Dulles was definitely not satisfied with Macmillan's answer, but said, "Harold, Ike does believe in, or is fascinated by, those things, but I am not going to tell him about *this* one. I have got to keep him focused on the conference. Enough distractions around here without this."

My Swiss detective friend whispered that nobody knew what "the thing in the air" was, but that they were checking. I said, "This business about the President and flying saucers and such—well, I'd appreciate it if you didn't put it in your report tonight." He just smiled, and I added, "Are you going to write a report on me *every* night?"

"Ah," he said, "but Monsieur Jefferson, we must be colleagues, friends."

Dulles had his finger in his whiskey and was ignoring Macmillan, who was staring out at the lake as I pressed the Swiss detective with, "What I am saying is that the President and flying saucers have nothing to do with your reports on me—reports I *know* you must write."

All innocence, he responded, "You do not think that I write such reports, do you?"

"Of course you do," I said, "but what I really want to know is, who reads them besides your superiors? The Soviets?"

He looked genuinely shocked. "Never."

"Only the Swiss?"

"Well," he said, thoughtfully, "I am Swiss, sooo . . . you see?"

"You are saying that I should draw my own conclusions?"

"Precisely."

Macmillan, behind us, came through with, "Well, Foster, in spite of Ike and his—migawd! flying saucers!—but, we *are* here, at the *summit*, aren't we?"

"Yes," Dulles said, through grinding peanuts, "Harold, we are here."

"Quite, Foster. Quite. And we're here despite those chaps out there who seem to think you are Ike. You *aren't* Ike, are you? You *are* you. Or . . . do you just appear to be you?"

"There is a subtle distinction, here, Harold," Dulles replied in his best deep bullfrog croak.

Macmillan gurgled some more words. "Nothing subtle about the distinction between you and Ike, Foster."

Dulles looked mean. "You have a way with words, Harold."

Macmillan's words became a series of hiccups. "For . . . better . . . or . . . er, uh . . . worse . . . er . . . Foster, that is, you, and Ike, and, well, all of us, we are all HERE, that is . . . at the summit."

Dulles eyed Macmillan strangely. "Well, yes, Harold . . . are you all right?"

"Quite."

"Yes, good. Changes. Ike's prestige . . ." Dulles' thoughts seemed disjointed. Shrouded in a towel and an old white hat, he said, "The point about Ike is, Harold, if they *see* too much of him here, will he still impress them all that much?—the mystery removed and that sort of thing."

Macmillan stared and then gave what proved to be the purest example of burble-speak that I was to hear. He said, "Foster, quite, that is—*some*body must see Ike so they'll know it really is him—but, erump, although, let's see, those police out there don't see Ike, they see, er, uh, *you*, although, of course, they may think that, uh, they see Ike because they've been *ordered* to see Ike, not you, so they may *understand* that it is you, but *know* that it is Ike, and—this can be dangerous around the Russians—but, there it is. You see?"

"My God, Harold!" Dulles sputtered. "Be serious!"

"I am quite serious, Foster."

"I'm not talking about the police!" Dulles said, his voice rising. "I'm talking about the Soviets, the French, and," with a small snicker, "you and your Prime Minister, Anthony Eden."

Macmillan's voice hiccuped along. "Quite so, Foster. Known Ike a long time, I have. During the war. All that. Yes, indeed . . ."

Dulles crunched some nuts and studied his friend the British Foreign Secretary. He liked, and, more importantly, respected Harold Macmillan, which was not the case with then British Prime Minister Anthony Eden. Dulles' dislike of Eden had bordered on being a case of dislike before first sight. With Macmillan, it was the opposite. He really liked Macmillan. He felt comfortable with Macmillan. He said, "Harold, the important thing is for you and me to keep in close touch."

"Absolutely, Foster, absolutely," Macmillan agreed.

The Swiss detective had hold of my shoulder. Words poured into my ear. "The boat is still asking if that is Eisenhower under the towel?"

"Haven't you told them it's Dulles?" I asked.

"No. Being uncertain keeps them on their toes."

"If you think that's best—okay," I said. "What about the flying saucer?"

"The unidentified aircraft? Yes. No news as yet, but we are checking."

"Please keep checking."

The detective hurried off to a radio car, presumably to keep checking.

Dulles was talking to Macmillan about patience. He said, "Harold, the Soviets start a negotiation as though it's already over, and they end a negotiation as though it is just beginning."

Macmillan was deep down in his chair, and I wondered

if he thought he was hiding, as he said, "With the Russians, negotiation never starts, and it never stops—it just goes on and on. As you said, 'patience.' Yes. But, you know, Foster, you have not exactly gotten yourself known for, uh . . . patience."

"Follow the flow of my *actions*, Harold," Dulles snorted, "*not* the sound of my words."

"Of course, Foster. But, words *are* important."

"Words are tools."

"Didn't Winston say that?"

"He may have."

"Quite," Macmillan murmured.

The actual summit started the next day. United Nations Secretary General Dag Hammarskjold met Eisenhower and Dulles at the entrance to the old League of Nations headquarters, the Palais des Nations, and deftly glided them past the mob of press, the public, and the curious. I remember Hammarskjold's walk as a slow, lunar motion. He seemed to be thinking through a poem rather than taking the President of the United States in to do verbal combat with the heirs to the Tsars.

The Soviets had arrived before us. When we entered the conference chamber, they all stood up and looked as though they were going to leave. I thought about Dulles' observation that they started a negotiation as if it was finished, but, instead of leaving, they surrounded Eisenhower. The short, flat-faced Soviet Defense Minister, Marshal Zhukov of World War II fame, embraced his old "comrade-in-arms," Dwight Eisenhower. Their awkward embrace drew over the short, rotund Party Secretary, Nikita Khrushchev, swinging his strong blacksmith's hands in every direction, and the goateed Soviet Premier, Marshal Nikolai Bulganin.

My attention was caught by Molotov's man, Colonel Alexandrov, who was standing stiffly to one side with two KGB colleagues, equally resplendent in their gleaming uniforms. The two new "Colonels" were the "security chiefs" for Khrushchev and Bulganin. I started toward them, but the British and the French came in and everybody sat down, composing their features for the photographers. The room was filled, but, for a moment, nobody, nothing—not even the photographers—moved. As a group, they were putting a paragraph in the history books, but looking at their faces—Soviet faces, French faces, English faces, American faces—you knew that each individual was living his own internal drama, trying to fit himself, alone, into the context of this historic event. It was a three-dimensional scene with more than three dimensions. Then Khrushchev laughed into Bulganin's ear, and history cranked up and got going once again. Everybody moved.

I walked back out of the conference room to the large hallway for a nicotine fix. After taking a few needed puffs, I glanced over at Colonel Alexandrov, who was eyeing me from the hall's other side, and started back down the narrow corridor. I was having my own little internal drama and I moved slowly. There was a similar corridor on the opposite side of the conference room. Each corridor had a small, curtained doorway about halfway down to its principal entrance to the room. By pulling one of those curtains aside, you could inconspicuously view the proceedings without actually entering the conference area. When I stopped and parted the curtains on my side, I found the eyes of Colonel Alexandrov peering straight at me from between the curtains directly opposite. I had just seen him in the hall, but gave it little thought. Eisenhower was talking about the dangers of surprise attack. I was struck by the President's obviously deep sincerity. When the time came for another cigarette, I walked back out to the hall, noticing Alexandrov's simultaneous arrival. We eyed each other. That was all. But, when, after fifteen minutes, I went back to take another look and, parting those "peeking" curtains, was again confronted with the owlish eyes and gleaming uniform of Colonel Alexandrov, something clicked in my head. I dropped the curtains suddenly and dashed back up the corridor. In the hall, Alexandrov came crashing through the other door, head churning, in search, apparently, for me. After satisfying himself that I was truly back in the hall, he took a deep breath, and, looking exhausted, dropped into an overstuffed chair.

I decided that it was time to end the game and walked over to him. We exchanged cigarettes, studied each other, nodded, stared, even smiled. His two colleagues, one large-shouldered and large-lipped, the other short, round, and limping, rushed over. They all talked to me, or at me. I couldn't understand a thing, but they were smiling. I talked back to them, or, perhaps, around them, and they didn't *seem* to understand me. But, we all began to laugh together, and I considered that a plus. To hold the jobs they held, I thought, they must be accomplished killers, so, better to have them laughing than doing otherwise.

When the conference session broke, I ducked back into the meeting room and grabbed up the stray bits of scratch paper, notes, doodles, and the like on the American side of the table. Eisenhower saw me, stopped dead in his tracks, and barked, "*What* are you *doing?*"

"Mr. President," I replied, "we pick up any notes and such that you and Secretary Dulles and the others make. There's a lot of paper here and we try to get it all." I should have stopped right there, but I added, "We don't always get it all, but we try."

Eisenhower grunted as only Eisenhower could grunt—a video grunt. If you soaked foam rubber in water and beat it with a tennis racquet, you would have the sound that came from his contorted face. He followed the grunt with a scowl, and a one word question. "*Why?*"

"Security reasons, sir," I replied.

"*What* in the *hell* kind of security?" he asked. His look was one that he must have used on West Point plebes when he was a First Classman.

"Mr. President," I said, exasperated, "if *we* don't pick the stuff up—secret papers, notes, doodles that show your thoughts—the Russians might."

Eisenhower's look turned to one of profound distaste. "The Russian security people are not picking *their* notes up. *They* are watching *you*."

It was true. The "Colonels" were all watching me. Eisenhower broke his frown with the famous grin, and said, "Maybe they just think you've got a good idea. The Russian generals used to copy *me* during the war." Then, he turned to look at Dulles across the room talking with some of the British, and, out of nowhere, asked me, "Just how many of those damned green suits *does* Foster have?"

Defensively, I said, "Brooks Brothers makes them for him."

"*That* is no excuse," Eisenhower grunted *(my God, what a grunt!)* and walked away.

I looked back over at the Russians. Eisenhower was right. They did think I had a good idea. They were grabbing everything in sight from their side of the table. One of them had his hand in a water pitcher, and I could see his fingers, magnified, moving like the tentacles of an octopus. Secret messages in a water pitcher? Unlikely. Still, maybe they knew something I didn't. Even so, I resisted stuffing my hand into our water pitcher.

In succeeding sessions, the Soviet security men made a game of racing me to the table. Generally, they had their side cleared of everything including water pitchers before I even got started. When they finished, they would stand watching me with big grins, as if to say, "We won! Ha!" *The Washington Post* described the Soviet attitude at this conference with considerable accuracy, I thought, as one of "ruthless amiability."

Sometimes, to escape that air of "ruthless amiability," I would leave Dulles and Eisenhower closeted in the meeting and slip outside for a breath of air. On one such occasion, I was hardly through the door when I found myself backed into a wall by a fat man with no hair and a baby-skin face, who, I thought, was there to kill me. Instead, he barked at me in uninflected English through a slit that served as his mouth, "America's a big pie with a lot left to be eaten, and if you are not careful, Eisenhower will let them eat it."

I started to argue, but Swiss policemen grabbed him and hustled him away. A Swiss detective smiled the words, "Monsieur Jefferson, you seem to attract odd people."

"I think it's Dulles who attracts them, not me," I replied.

"Perhaps it is something about the two of you together."

"Hell," I grouched, "I'm just his security man."

"I know." The detective shrugged. "All very unusual."

"*I'm* unusual?" I asked.

"No, no," he said. "Just not, uh, typical."

I wanted to pursue that conversation, but Dulles came through the door, and I leaped to find the car.

When we returned the following morning, I found myself once again playing "up-and-down-the-corridor" and "I spy" with Colonel Alexandrov. Happily, he eventually tired of this strange game. He would not, however, let me get too far away without appearing close by. It was interesting, amusing, but not disturbing, and I didn't have time to worry about it anyway. My mind was in the middle of what the press described as the "Black Snow" crisis. Black flakes were descending on Geneva, and America was being blamed. One Swiss told me that there was a widely held belief that only America had the technological capability for such "magic." Besides, the heaviest concentrations were emanating from the vicinity of

U.S. headquarters in the du Rhône hotel. Determined inquiry traced the source not to the heavens or to some infernal machine, but to a single Hotel du Rhône chimney—the chimney beneath which all American paper containing "Secret" information was burned.

The Swiss were indignant, claiming the spreading of this "Black Snow" in Swiss "air space" was a violation of their "neutrality." The Soviets screamed "imperialist plot." I myself had absolutely nothing to do with this infringement of Swiss neutrality. However, I *was* John Foster Dulles' personal security officer and, therefore, considered by many to be the likely culprit. So, there I was, with the ever-present Colonel Alexandrov watching, trying to explain to a group of reporters why America saw fit to bring its "Black Snow" to Switzerland, while, at that very moment, Dulles was telling Molotov that the United States "had no 'Secrets'"—that only the Soviet Union had "Secrets." One reporter went directly from me to Dulles and screamed at him "YOU *BURN* YOUR SECRETS AND BRING THEM DOWN OVER SWITZERLAND!!!"

Dulles peered through his spectacles at the screaming reporter, sniffing as if seeking a scent. Then, he said, very calmly, "Yes, *our* secrets are in the air for all to see, while Soviet secrets lie in a darkness none of us will ever penetrate."

"What about your brother?" another reporter asked. "What about Allen Dulles?"

Dulles laughed. "My brother has been after me to explain our 'secrets in the air,' which, he says, are therefore not secrets."

The reporter did not think that it was funny. His words chopped out like an ax hitting wood. *"What do you mean?"*

Dulles looked over at me. I said, "It is my understanding that our 'Black Snow' has been gathered by the Soviets and is on its way to Moscow at this very moment." My tongue was in my cheek.

Dulles jumped in with, "So, you see, no secrets . . ."

The reporter was confused and not happy. He said, "The Soviets state that they have irrefutable proof that the secret paper you are burning is impregnated with fire-resistant poison that is now spreading out over Switzerland." *His* tongue was not in his cheek.

It seemed outrageous, but, actually, the Soviets were already indulging in a great deal of spiritual taxidermy— stuffing people's heads with all manner of thoughts and ideas that were not there before. Of course, if you know what they are doing, you can defend yourself, and sometimes have some fun. When Alexandrov, through an interpreter, asked me, "Why is America shipping its germs to the Soviet Union?" I came right back with, "In the hope that you will send us back our own germs instead of all those exotic and deadly viruses you are now trying out on us."

It was the next day that we—more accurately, I—really got down to it. The Soviets held a luncheon at their villa for the leaders of the other delegations, but Eisenhower, as the only Chief of State at the conference, followed protocol and did not attend. Protocol said that the Premiers and Foreign Ministers could go to him, but that he could not go to them. So, the British and French leaders were there, and Dulles acted for Eisenhower.

It was early afternoon when we pulled into the Soviet villa's shrubbery-shrouded and heavily guarded grounds. Dulles went right in. I stayed outside with the Scotland Yard men accompanying the British, and the French and Swiss detectives, trying to decide where I might eat. The decision was made for me. Anthony Eden's Yard man sidled over to me and, nodding toward some of the Soviet security men, whispered in my ear, "Hold tight, old boy. The Russkies have a real meal set on for us."

Fine, I thought. But, as I looked over at stone-faced "General" Zhakarov, ostensible chief of Soviet security, and, as everyone continued to stand around, looking each other over, kicking gravel, whispering furtively, I wondered when this notable event—this "real meal"—was going to take place.

The Russians were all standing very still, ignoring the British, French, and Swiss, and staring directly at me—probably because I was the only American. I kicked some gravel. They kicked some gravel. Everybody started kicking gravel. Nobody moved, except to kick gravel. I looked down a hill in the gravel drive, and saw our embassy driver from Berne (he was Swiss) parking our limousine and felt reassured. Then, one of the Russians made a sign of some sort, and there was general movement up a narrow forest path. I walked with the Yard men. The eyes of the Russians were still on me. It was strange. We were, quite literally, in the woods. Dulles was safe enough, but *what*, I asked myself, was I doing in the woods with the KGB? Then, we were out of the woods, confronted by a second villa. It was large, old, well-hidden, and with, apparently, no means of motorized access.

When we entered the imposing expansiveness of this nineteenth-century relic, we were quietly ushered to a large table laden with caviar, sturgeon, fish of all sorts, cheeses, salads, cold cuts, and, of course, vodka, cognac, and wine.

We sat in fine old wicker chairs, with "General" Zhakarov acting as host. Everyone quietly set to. The Soviets continued to eye me, not much interested in anyone else. My ego was in good enough shape that I had no trouble grasping the reason—it wasn't me, but the flag I walked under. Stalin's famous question came to mind. When told of the moral power of the Pope, he asked how many divisions the Pope controlled? I was the only American at the table, and between the Americans, the British, and the French, the Soviets knew who had the divisions.

There was little talk. The Russians kept studying me. I

studied them back. They were all in civilian clothes. When they had seen that they were the only uniformed security men at the conference, they had taken their uniforms off, but they appeared to miss them. They kept fiddling with their shirt collars, yanking, jerking, and twisting. Scowls alternated with smiles, smiles with scowls. They ate rapidly. Eating was serious business. So was drinking, and, as more and more bottles were emptied, the "Spirit of Geneva" gradually began to take over. The toasts began. A devious process. One of the Russians would raise his glass, and a Russian-speaking Swiss detective would translate it into French. Next, an English-speaking Swiss detective assigned to the British would translate it into English. Then, the whole process would go into reverse. On the advice of two of my colleagues from Scotland Yard, I joined in each round with only a light sip. The vodka was potent, more potent than the Alabama moonshine that had been my yardstick since army service in Alabama at age eighteen.

At first, the toasts, one after another, consisted of innocuous generalities about "peace."

"To peace."

"To world peace."

"To peace between the Soviet Union and the United States."

"To peace between the United States and the Soviet Union."

"To peace between the Soviet Union, the United States, and all the peace-loving nations of the world."

"To peace between Switzerland, the United States, France, the Soviet Union, the United Kingdom, and all the peace-loving nations of the world."

"To peace between the United Kingdom, the Soviet Union, Switzerland, the United States, and France."

It went on and on until one of my Yard friends, Teddy Wrenn, a former British Army boxing champion about whom Shakespeare would have written, if he had known him, stood up and proposed a toast to "Peace between men and women." After it went through the ponderous interpreting process, our hosts looked dumbfounded. The question was all over their faces—"What does he *really* mean?" I was sitting next to Teddy, and all Soviet eyes turned on me as if *I* might be responsible for something deep and threatening. Teddy just stood there with his glass held high. The Russians all began talking to each other at once, and then everybody was laughing and they were all pointing at me as I felt something large, globular, and soft pressing into the back of my head. It was a woman's posterior. I stood up and she turned around and I found myself facing a female of truly imposing proportions wrapped in a plain uniform. She was sniffing— "sniff, sniff, sniff"—and her pudgy nose tilted upward as if she was sniffing for the scent of God, or so I thought at the vodka-influenced time. She lowered the nose, exhaled a dose of garlic-filled breath, which appeared to be colored yellow, pinched my cheek, and disappeared. The KGB men already gathered around me began punching me in the shoulders. They seemed to like to pinch, punch, and poke. Little did I realize that this was but the beginning.

Teddy Wrenn was still on his feet, clanking glasses with his Yard colleague, Erich Carr. Everybody drank to him, and "peace between men and women," and the whole toasting process was tracked again with the Russians' sentiments becoming ever more friendly—almost too friendly, and sweet, to be real. Responding in kind was like eating chewy toffee.

On and on it went, but, finally, Anthony Eden's Yard Inspector, Terry Austin, rose, glass thrust forward, aimed at "General" Zhakarov, and proposed a toast to our hosts—"To *Premier Bulganin* and to *Party Secretary Khrushchev!*" As his words were going through the interpreting process, the other Yard men and the lone French detective got to their feet. I was already standing. The Swiss detectives got up. But the Russians, who were mostly already standing, sat down, and those few still seated remained in their seats. They looked stunned, agitated. Their nerves showed. The wizened little "Colonel" with a limp, who traveled with Khrushchev and who had been whispering in "General" Zhakarov's ear, was spitting his whispers. Then, suddenly, he smiled—a small smile that reminded me of a rubber band under tension. Zhakarov, twice the little "Colonel's" size, seemed to be bowing to him in spirit if not in body. The "General's" cheeks jumped around as if a mosquito had got loose inside his mouth. But, in between attempts to smile back at the little "Colonel," he managed to get to his feet. Holding his glass near the table, he spoke, softly, to the Russian-speaking Swiss detective. When his words got through the complicated interpreting process and the verbal minuet was concluded, we learned that we did *not* owe our thanks to "Premier Bulganin and Party Secretary Khrushchev," but to "Comrade Party Secretary Khrushchev and Comrade Premier Bulganin" *in that order.*

Glasses clanked. But the stress among the Russians over what had seemed to be a friendly and harmless toast, in keeping with protocol, lent an air of bewilderment to the whole thing. Zhakarov had taken on the look of someone suffering severe constipation. He continued to play the host, but he certainly was not the top Soviet security man present. Khrushchev's "Colonel" who called himself something that sounded like "Yatselev" (most of them had many "work" names), was a more likely candidate. Indeed, after the conference I learned that he was in fact a deputy chief of the entire KGB and a general rather than a colonel. Not only did they have many names, but their ranks were rarely real. Dealing with them was like being the centerpiece in a jigsaw puzzle. You kept trying to figure out what fit where around you, but you could never see all the pieces, and some that you saw came from another puzzle. When I told Dulles and some of our Soviet "experts" about the tension over the toast, they were struck by the fact that Khrushchev was put before Bulganin because, at that time, nobody was sure who was really in charge in the Soviet Union. In the more protocol-conscious luncheons and dinners of the higher echelons, lip service was paid to the "position" of Premier Bulganin, but, in the more pragmatic, directly power-conscious circles of the KGB, the real boss, Nikita Khrushchev, came first.

So, we toasted Khrushchev and Bulganin, and Eisenhower, and Eisenhower and Dulles, and Eisenhower and Khrushchev and Bulganin, and Prime Minister Eden, and Khrushchev and Bulganin, and French Premier Faure, and Switzerland, and Eisenhower and Khrushchev and peace, and peace and Khrushchev and Eisenhower. I really got into it, jumping up and down with toasts, and, each time, having a Russian jump right back at me with a deft response. It was like playing tennis with a slightly better player and constantly having the ball fired back at you. Then, one of the Russians, with a broad smile showing bad teeth, told what can only be described as a dirty joke, and, as it went into the interpreting process, he started on another. The party was disintegrating from peace to pornography when we were interrupted by word that the "big" luncheon was breaking up. As we all started back down the path toward the main villa, the Swiss detectives assured me that Dulles' car would be brought up in plenty of time. Other limousines were already pulling up and pulling out. The British took off. The French were milling around. It was warm. The humidity was thick, like gauze. Dulles came out wiping his brow. Khrushchev's collar was soaked with sweat. Bulganin looked a little cooler. Not much. He had this automatic smile that came and went like the up-and-down mouth of a ventrilo-

quist's dummy. Everybody was talking, not really understanding each other—the interpreter couldn't keep up.
There was laughter. Everything seemed fine, except that
our Cadillac limousine with its American flag up front
was nowhere to be seen. I jogged down the hill to the
parking lot. The Cadillac was there, but the Swiss driver
had disappeared, *with* the keys. Was it a conspiracy, I
asked myself? Or a savage joke on *me* by the KGB? My
future at that moment seemed like a bubble ready to
burst. Then I spotted another limousine with an American
delegation sticker *and* a driver sitting comfortably behind
the wheel. I leaped in beside him with "last chance"
eagerness, and totally tore apart his hard-earned
Swiss-French serenity when I bellowed in my very best
very-loud-English, "You are driving Dulles now! DULLES!
DULLES! LET'S GO! *VITE!*"

The man was terrified. *"Non, non,"* he said. "I drive
Monsieur Harold Stassen."

"TO HELL WITH HAROLD STASSEN!" I shouted.

Stassen was at the conference to advise Eisenhower on
disarmament, and it was my firm intention to disarm him
of his automobile. The driver did not seem to understand
my priorities. So, I pulled out my rarely used Security
Officer's badge (a shield that looked good but meant little)
and roared, *"Police! Policier! Police!"* That did it. He
started the engine as I egged him on with, "Dulles! Dulles!
Vite! Police! *Vite!*"

Up the hill we chugged, into the drive by the villa. Dulles, still standing with Khrushchev and Bulganin, turned
toward me as I leaped from my commandeered car. I
rushed to him, elbowing the Soviet leaders out of the way,
gargling out words like "No driver . . . no car . . . 'nother
car . . . 's okay, *our* driver's gone but 's okay . . ."

Dulles looked at me like I'd come in by parachute. But
he listened and, after a couple of hiccupping laughs, he

asked Khrushchev and Bulganin, through an interpreter, "What did you do, get my chauffeur drunk?"

The KGB men, standing close by, kept interrupting the interpreter, and the Soviet leaders looked puzzled at first. Then they looked at me and drowned out Dulles' small laugh with large laughs of their own. The "Colonels" were all laughing, too. I was not laughing. I grabbed Harold Stassen and offered him a ride in his own car. I don't think he heard me. I thought he was going to ask me to vote for him. I backed away. The "Colonels" were all wagging their fingers at me, and, when they saw me talking to Stassen, they wagged their fingers at him, and he beamed, putting his much-used "vote-seeking" techniques into operation on them, grabbing their hands and shoulders and wrists—he went for one neck, but the KGB officer, a man with an already dented frame, ducked—all the while saying, "Glad to see ya', glad to see ya,'" and so on, and on. He baffled the "Colonels" and they shrunk back from him, aiming their fingers at me, and saying something that sounded like "Tut, tut. Tut, tut. Tut, tut, tut . . ." Dulles, trying to ignore Stassen, stage-whispered in my ear, "Okay, Lou, let's make our getaway." Then, as if remembering something long forgotten, he turned to Stassen and, his voice rising, asked, "Harold, do you want a ride?" Stassen's neck was moving, but his head was still. I think that he had finally grasped the fact that he was being "offered" a ride in his own vehicle, but before he could say anything, Livingston Merchant gave him a push, and we all piled into the car with me shouting *"VITE! VITE!"* to the driver. On our way out, the Soviet leaders waved and pointed, and one of the KGB men did a dance.

About five minutes after our return to the Palais for the afternoon meeting, Dulles' limousine, with driver, pulled in. When my anger cut through the alcoholic haze that surrounded him, the driver slurred out a story about going to lunch and the Russians not letting him back in until it was too late.

The Swiss police thought that it was simply a KGB prank. Some of our own intelligence people saw something more sinister, because I think they wanted to see something more sinister. I inclined toward the Swiss view, which just made me mad—not angry mad, but mad mad. I vowed within myself to get even.

When the Soviets arrived for the afternoon session, I was standing with all the other gawkers in a hallway. *Les Russes* put on quite a show each day as they marched in, two by two—Khrushchev and Bulganin, Molotov and Zhukov, Gromyko and so on down the line. Like just about everybody else there, I found them quite entertaining and watched them whenever I could. When they arrived at my vantage point, Khrushchev stopped, and they all followed suit. There was wonder, and fear, on their faces. Something must be wrong. To stop was not in the accepted pattern. They stood like statues, but Khrushchev waddled over to me, laughing (one observer described his laugh as sounding like "a horse having an orgasm") and shouting in Russian. He started to punch me lightly in the stomach. The punches came in harder. Then, he pinched my cheek. His protruding stomach backed me close into the wall, and the rest of the Russians surrounded me, pointing, clucking, laughing, wagging their heads. Then, very suddenly, Khrushchev turned serious and did an about face, and they all turned serious and did an about face and continued their march down the hall.

The hall, full of people, was quiet as I watched their backs disappear. All eyes were on me.

When I asked a Russian-speaking Swiss detective what Khrushchev had been shouting at me, he said, "The Party Secretary was telling you that he was happy that the, uh,

'unpredictable' er, uh, Mr. Dulles had not shot you for losing his car."

"Shot me, or *had* me shot?" I asked.

The Swiss detective thought a moment. "He seemed to
believe that Mr. Dulles might, shall we say, have personally . . . shot you."

"Was he serious?" I asked.

"I certainly thought so." The detective paused, then continued, "He said, I think, that perhaps he did not understand Mr. Dulles' *true* character after all, that he had been
convinced that it was in Mr. Dulles' nature to *personally*
dispose of you for causing an, uh, inconvenience."

The mind doesn't take in things like that immediately—
at least my mind doesn't. I repeated the question.
"Khrushchev was *really* serious?"

"Certainly."

Dulles was incredulous when I told him of Khrushchev's alleged reaction, but he took to calling me his
"celebrity" after remarking, "Lou, how many people—
Americans—do you think have been pinched on the cheek
and punched in the stomach by Nikita Khrushchev after
having been rumored to have been executed by the hand
of John Foster Dulles? Why, you must have been like a
resurrection to Khrushchev. My heavens, you may have
even given him religion. That would be historic. Indeed,
you may well be unique in history."

The next day, we went back to the Soviet villa for another luncheon—a luncheon in Dulles' honor. The British
and the French weren't invited. It was just "them and us."
Before we arrived, Dulles looked at the driver he had told
me should have a "second chance" and then said to me,
"Lou, it does seem that we ought to have our driver here,
today," adding, with a twinkle, "Harold Stassen won't be
at this luncheon, you know."

My reply was to the point. "He'll be here."

The KGB "Colonels" were all watching as, once again,

we splashed up the gravel of the Soviet villa's driveway. They gathered around me, grinning, as I gave the driver one final lecture on the importance of being present. Then, when he tried to move the limousine to one side of the drive, they blocked him, waving their arms, pointing, laughing, jeering, like school children. It was hard to believe that they were KGB "killers"—very high-ranking ones at that. I even felt sorry for the driver as he edged the car over, stopped the engine, and slunk down deeply into the seat. With a few final jeers, the "Colonels" gave it up and beckoned me over to a picnic table laden with food and drink. All very friendly. The "*Spirit* of Geneva." Khrushchev's "Colonel" began fixing me fish sandwiches and slapping me on the back, while instructing the bilingual Swiss detectives to tell me how much the Soviet Union wanted peace with the United States. I told them, as I munched my fish sandwiches, to tell him how much the United States wanted peace with the Soviet Union. We all clanked glasses. Then I asked the Russian-speaking Swiss detective to ask Khrushchev's man if he had gotten our driver drunk the day before. When my question was translated, the Russians as a group began chanting one of the few English words they admitted understanding— "No, no, no, no, no, no, no, no, no, no, no . . ." They were, at the same time, pressing boxes of cigarettes and bottles of vodka into my hands, and it crossed my mind that they were all acting "guilty" as hell. I let it drop, for the moment, and took some food—no drink—over to our Swiss driver. He was sitting as if he was standing at attention. When I gave him the food, he thanked me profusely. Tears rolled down from his eyes. I was embarrassed. I told him that it was the "Spirit of Geneva." Even so, I was still thinking of the events of the day before, and the Soviets remained on a very big hook in my mind.

That night, at the request of an FBI agent I knew and liked, and who just "happened" to be in Geneva, I visited one of the Soviet delegation offices that I had been in and out of with Dulles. I had had a chance to size the place up and was the only American security or intelligence officer who had had such an opportunity. The one Soviet guard was in the front, and I slipped in a side entrance, bringing out a complete list of the Soviet delegation—a list that all the various Western intelligence services had been trying, without success, to obtain. I gave a copy to my grateful friend from the FBI, who sent it on to J. Edgar Hoover, who, I am sure, enjoyed leaking the fact of his exclusive ownership of the much sought after list. I knew that this was so when, almost immediately, CIA people I didn't even know existed appeared, and became friendly, with respect in their eyes. I probably diluted that respect when I answered the question of how I "did it" by making it all sound simple. Part of the game in those days—these days, too, I suspect—was to make the simple sound complex. But, I said, "Well, I'd already been in the place, and the United Nations guards knew my face, and I didn't see any Russians around, and I knew the right door to go through, and I was kinda' mad at those KGB types, and, no, I did not have to pick any locks because the door I went through was open [I had flipped the lock earlier and it was still flipped], and, yes, the lists were right there on a desk where I'd seen them when I'd been in the place with Secretary Dulles, so, I just grabbed them, and got out in a hurry. Never did see any Russians."

It really was awfully easy, and I wondered about that. A Foreign Service Officer from our London Embassy speculated that the Soviets believed that we were too "polite" to do anything so "nefarious." When I wisecracked that "Gentlemen do not read other gentlemen's mail!" he, very seriously, agreed, repeating sternly, "Gentlemen do *not* read other gentlemen's mail."

A little irritated, I said, "*They* are certainly not gentlemen, and I am not *altogether* sure about us."

Obviously offended, this young man responded in a huff, "*Speak* for yourself."

"Besides," I said, "I didn't steal any mail."

"We must have rules and we must adhere to them!" he sniffed. He reminded me of a mechanical dog that, wherever you put him, would just keep going around and around, but I wondered about his idea that the Soviets thought we were just too "polite" to steal their "secrets." Certainly they knew better than that.

Another theory, which made more sense to me, was that the Soviets "*wanted*" us to have the lists and they wanted us to attach more importance to them than they deserved. The whole thing could have been meant to merely add to our confusion. I got a strong reaction when I voiced this idea to some of our security and intelligence contingents. The FBI did not want to believe it, and the CIA just refused to believe it. I was not sure what I believed, but I knew that I felt better about the lost limousine, and Nikita Khrushchev's punch to my solar plexus.

So, there you have an example of intelligence gathering for the United States government. When I told Dulles about it, he said, "Heroic, Lou, heroic . . . a little more motivation and no telling what you are apt to do."

"Is that a compliment?" I asked.

"Of sorts," he said. "Of sorts."

He seemed to find the whole business fascinating, but I didn't tell him—at that time—about the beautiful young woman in my room at the Hotel du Rhône, who, when I entered it the day after my "grand theft," began to take her clothes off. In heavily accented English, she announced that she was going to take a bath because she had just gotten a job in the du Rhône as a maid after crossing Lake Geneva that morning on "se wrung boot" (that is approximately the way she said it) and . . . I stopped her right there and pointed at the door. I couldn't believe it. I had just been talking to my FBI friend about

THE JOHN FOSTER DULLES BOOK OF HUMOR

the American security officer in Moscow who had been "set up" by a "gorgeous" woman who received her pay checks from the KGB. I told my half-clothed visitor, "You may be the Lady of the Lake, but you have got to leave."

She appeared confused over "Lady of the Lake" and startled that I wanted her to leave. More than that, she seemed scared. Five feet away, I could hear her heart going "kerthump, kerthump." After I helped her to dress and gave her a little push toward the door, she gave me an odd look, the look of someone who has seen the same movie too many times, and she grasped the doorknob so tightly that her knuckles turned white. But she did leave.

I closed the door quickly behind her and checked around my room. At first, I thought that all of my belongings were intact. Then, I noticed that my list of the U.S. delegation to the conference was missing. I was irritated. It was a public document, given to the press. But *that* copy was mine. Damnit! Then I wondered, was this whole thing some kind of symbolic theft?

I was angry over what appeared to be a cat-and-mouse game with the KGB, but I didn't mention that fact to a KGB officer, with a press relations cover, who, later that day, over drinks, commented to me, "When you Americans are pushed, you are hard fighters, relentless . . . but, only when you *know* you are being pushed." After two more of those lethal little vodka shots, he added, "Yes, and you Americans have a need to see yourselves in control . . . that can be used." He was excited. I tried to argue, but he laughed at me. Not with me. At me. I can still hear that awful laugh. It had a sound like soft raw meat hitting a hot frying pan. Then he pinched my cheek (they all seemed to be into cheek pinching), saying (or predicting), "When your children and your grandchildren are in the streets with bombs, you will know what it is to feel *out* of control, but *they* will feel *in* control, and that, my friend, is the joke. So, drink, my friend, drink!"

Years later, a member of the staff of the old U.S. Senate Internal Security Subcommittee showed me a picture of a KGB paymaster for terrorists. It was the man with the raw-meat laugh.

At the time, I told Dulles that a KGB officer thought we were "hard fighters" but that we had a need to be in "control" of everything.

Dulles snorted back with, "Control, huh! As long as they never question our will to fight, whenever, wherever, however necessary. That's the key. That's the way not to *have* to fight . . . well . . . at least, on any large scale. You always have to be ready to stand up when they give you the wrong kind of . . . nudge. Hah! I know, people say I'm bloodthirsty." He laughed. "I'm not bloodthirsty, but I hope the Soviets never stop thinking I am." He pulled out his pocketknife, started to sharpen a pencil, and went on, "When I do this—sharpen pencils with a knife—at that conference table, it makes Molotov nervous. He watches. It distracts him. He fidgets, but he watches. Guess it fits my 'bloodthirsty' image. Khrushchev even asked Chip Bohlen why I carry a knife."

"You don't mind it if the Soviets think you're bloodthirsty?" I asked.

"Keeps them cautious in their expansionist moves," he replied, adding, "makes them more willing to think about things like disarmament. If we act weak, it will only encourage their aggression."

"Well, Mr. Secretary," I said, "if anybody asks *me*, I'll tell 'em that's not a pocketknife you carry, but a claw— the eagle's claw!"

He smiled, but his words came gravel-crunching out, "Why don't you tell that to those big Russian bodyguards who seem to spend more time watching you than they do watching Khrushchev and Molotov, which is what they are supposed to be doing, isn't it?"

Good question.

I replied, "Sure, but anything we Americans do seems to fascinate them, and that's probably part of their job, too, to pick up anything they can from us Americans. Besides, those guys are *really* 'bloodthirsty'!"

Dulles' eyes twitched. He gave them an extra twitch when he growled, "More 'bloodthirsty' than I am?"

He was in good form. I played along. "All of their worst suspicions would be confirmed if they knew you had a pearl-handled .38-caliber Smith & Wesson revolver given to you by a Central American dictator."

The twitch turned to a twinkle. "Good Lord, yes, that would do it, wouldn't it? It's at home, of course, but . . . maybe I'll tell 'em! Wouldn't *that* be something! Still, I don't know. I've had that revolver for thirty-five years and I really was on a diplomatic mission to Costa Rica for President Wilson when President Tinoco—I guess you could call him a dictator—gave it to me—to protect myself. And that reminds me! You'd better get my license renewed when we get back to Washington."

"You carrying?" I asked.

His laugh got his stomach shaking. It sounded like it was coming up out of the bottom of a volcano. He said, "I told you that it's at home, but, my heavens, I hope *you* are, how did you put it . . . carrying?"

I patted the .38 "Bodyguard" on my hip and responded, "Of course, I am, but, Mr. Secretary, you *know* you don't *need* a license in the District of Columbia like you did in New York—unless, of course, you *are* going to 'carry' . . ."

"No, I'm not going to 'carry,' as you put it," he said, thoughtfully. "But, maybe I *will* tell the Soviets about my license to carry a gun."

Which, in a way, he did, when, after the Geneva "summit" the Soviets claimed that our fingerprinting of Soviet citizens when they entered the U.S. did not promote the "Spirit of Geneva." Dulles scoffed at this and told a press conference that there was "nothing to" fingerprinting; that he got "fingerprinted every year" when he renewed his permit to keep a revolver. This statement created a real press storm. One writer even translated it into, "John Foster Dulles admits handgun possession—he must be stopped."

Dulles' comment on that was, "Some of them will criticize *any*thing I do, but we do seem to have gone from atom bombs to pistols. Maybe that's a form of progress."

"Hey," I said, "Eisenhower and Khrushchev with pistols at high noon on Main Street."

"The President would win!" Dulles chuckled.

"How do you know?" I asked. "Because he's a general?"

"He was born in Texas."

"You think that would do it?"

"Yes," Dulles said, happily. "Lord, wouldn't that be something—if we could start taking war backward, step by step."

"We'd be making progress by replacing atom bombs with TNT and TNT with the Colt .45, and, so on."

He really liked the idea and kept it going with, "We'd be going forward by going backward."

"What about all the bombs?" I asked.

"Well," he said, "maybe we could have a bomb exchange."

"Have it by a great big ditch."

The thought appealed to him, and he repeated, "By a ditch!" and then added, wistfully, "If only it was possible."

Eisenhower's last speech at the Geneva summit was not, however, on pistols and ditches, but on the dangers of "surprise attack." There was a great roar of thunder as he began, and the lights in the elaborate conference room went out. It was only a simple power failure, but one of the suspicious "Colonels" asked the Swiss police if I could have had anything to do with it? A reporter heard about the Soviet suspicion and asked me if I had switched the lights to dramatize the "whole surprise attack thing—

make it look like a surprise attack, and all that?" This got back to Dulles, who said that I was "now assuming" what he described as "legendary proportions."

Even Eisenhower came up to me and said, "Congratulations"—I was never totally clear on that—but then he turned to Dulles and said, "Foster, I really think we can score some points on the Soviets with our 'Open Skies' proposal. Hell, they don't want everybody flying around looking at everybody else, so they'll say 'no' and we've *scored!*"

"Scored?" Dulles questioned.

"World opinion," Eisenhower said. "In the great arena of world opinion, we will have scored on the Soviets— something we rarely do."

"Harold Stassen thinks that you really believe in the 'Open Skies' idea. So does Nelson Rockefeller."

"*I do believe in it*, Foster, but the Russians don't. They'll say 'no' and keep right on with their armaments, and we'll have to stay ahead of them, and God knows where it will all end. It's frightening, but we can't delude ourselves."

"True, Mr. President, but, suppose, eventually, they say 'yes' to 'Open Skies' or disarmament?" Dulles asked, softly.

"Not in my planning!" Eisenhower snapped, darting around Dulles like a fly in a bottle.

Dulles ducked, as if he thought the President was going to hit him, but said, "We must come to grips with the arms issue, but . . ."

"Ex*act*ly," Eisenhower said, turning his attention elsewhere.

As Dulles and I walked away, the Secretary stage-whispered, "Lou, I may have to borrow those 'legendary proportions' of yours if I am to continue dealing with the President."

I told him that *he* was the legend, not me.

"I don't want to be a legend," he replied. "I am merely trying to keep the world safe for those who do."

7

More to This Than Being Pinched by Khrushchev

As time went on, I sometimes found myself feeling more like a fool than a legend. "Things" just seemed to "happen."

After Eisenhower told the British and French to end their 1956 invasion of Suez (a response to Egyptian President Nasser's Suez Canal takeover), dealing with the diplomats of those two old allies came to resemble visits to a deep freeze. Dulles recalled visiting a meat-packing plant during his ill-fated 1949 New York campaign for the U.S. Senate and sailing Lake Ontario in the winter, but said that he had never felt anything quite like the chill of that meat-packing plant until the Suez crisis. It made him angry. He felt that the British in particular were "underestimating" Eisenhower, that they were trying to "shame him because of old associations," but, Dulles said, "it won't work, because President Eisenhower thinks *they* are the ones who should be ashamed."

More to This Than Being Pinched by Khrushchev

During this "cold spell," we flew to New York for a United Nations special session, and Britain's Harold Macmillan, Selwyn Lloyd, and Lord Hood visited Dulles and his top aides in the State Department's Waldorf Towers suite. As he came in, Macmillan had the somber air of a man arriving at a funeral. Selwyn Lloyd would have made a good funeral director. Hood was another matter. He was one of those British aristocrats whose ice-cutter nose dominated his face, whatever his feelings. Dulles escorted them into the small drawing room, where they sat down and stared at one another. You could *feel* the silence. I stood just inside the hall door. The silence had an hypnotic effect. Macmillan kept raising his feet off the floor as if he was afraid they might get wet. I thought of reminding him that the Suez Canal was in Egypt. I didn't. Dulles interrupted my thoughts with, "Lou! Drinks! Get some ice!"

I dashed into the suite's small kitchen and found some ice cubes in the refrigerator, dumped them into a bowl, and, bowl clutched to my bosom, dashed back, slipped, and, with ice cubes flying in air, fell flat on my face somewhere between Harold Macmillan and John Foster Dulles.

Most of the cubes came down over Macmillan, lubricating his moustache and landing in his lap. I was flat out and face down on the floor, my eyes studying the rug, my ears listening for some break in the silence, my mind feeling like a word in a sentence written by someone else. Then, Macmillan gave a small, shaky, and tentative laugh, muttering, "I say, Foster, what's that chap of yours doing on the floor?"

Lord Hood chimed in with, "Yes, yes, I say, strange . . . what?"

Everybody laughed.

I stood up.

The laughter got louder.

I started picking ice cubes off Macmillan. He said to Dulles, "I say, Foster, you didn't *order* him to, er, throw ice at me? . . . ho, ho . . . did you?"

Dulles choked over some unintelligible words as Macmillan added, "Well, we can add that—ice bombardment—to the agenda of things we just must discuss."

I backed out of the room.

Later, when I apologized to Dulles for hurling ice cubes at the British, he patted me on the shoulder—sort of the way I had seen him pat his poodle, Pepin—and said, "That's all right, Lou, you broke the ice in more ways than one."

Relieved that he was taking it in such good humor, I said, "I guess it *was* more of an accomplishment than when I lost your passport in Paris."

"Ah, the passport," Dulles responded. "The French are still puzzled by that. They were convinced that there had to be something deep and sinister there, that it couldn't be anything so simple as a misplaced passport. This ice cube affair is much more straight forward."

The passport in question had slipped down behind one of the seats of our aircraft, but, for a full day, I had thought that it had been lost or stolen somewhere in Paris. Because it had seemed so personally embarrassing (I could see the headline—JOHN FOSTER DULLES' SECURITY MAN LOSES SECRETARY'S PASSPORT IN PARIS), I told my friends in the French police only part of the story. I asked them to look for a "very important document pertaining to the Secretary" that was "not where it should be in the Embassy residence," but, I assured them, they would "know it if they saw it." My reasoning, if it can be called that, was that if they found the passport, I would gladly take the embarrassment, but, if they didn't find it, I would, at least, avoid an international red face. Statesmanlike thinking? Of course. I didn't tell Dulles about it, either, hoping against hope I wouldn't have to. On one of our stops, as we traveled around Paris on that, for me, stressful day, I remember thinking that if I had, in truth, lost his passport, then Dulles was not legally in Paris, although he was, at that very moment, talking to the Premier of France. My fear made a quantum leap. Suppose Dulles found out! To someone with his legal turn of mind, the news that his passport had disappeared might well prove the worst about me and provoke consequences too terrible to contemplate. What a day it was. Even the air had an unreal quality, and I could see little mirages dancing in the sun, or were they in my head? But we kept moving. Dulles would go into a meeting, and I would rush to a phone, calling the police, intelligence agencies, Phyllis Bernau (I had confided in her and in Mrs. Dulles), asking for news, and trying to locate our pilot, who had the keys to our aircraft. Then, around noon, the police came up with someone they described as an "Algerian assassin" with connections in New York and Argentina. They had found him sticking pins into and burning little portions of a picture of Dulles. It was not his passport picture. When I asked if there was any significance to the pairing of New York and Argentina, they said "of course" and left it at that. Our consultation was interrupted when the pilot turned up in what he called an "unmarked hotel." He was in "hiding" with a woman he later described as being "three-handed" (actually, she reported to Polish intelligence, and worked for the French police, who knew she reported to Polish intelligence and, through the Poles, to the Soviets). In any event, his obscenities were choice when I told him that he would have to interrupt what must have been an unusual athletic contest and drive to the aircraft. He balked, but I got him going when I suggested that he ask his companion who her employers were.

After I found the passport behind the aircraft seat, I thanked the French police and intelligence people and told them the problem had been resolved. I tried to ignore Dulles, but he took one look at me after my return from the aircraft and said, "*Boy!* You look relieved! You must have found my passport."

"How did you know?" I whispered, my terror subsiding with his smile.

"Janet—Mrs. Dulles—told me. She was worried about you."

I was touched. Janet Dulles and I had become friends. We talked a lot. She once said to me over a late night drink, "Lou, when you and Foster go to all these places, meetings, conferences, and such, he comes back and tells me what Nehru or Winston Churchill or the Japanese Foreign Minister had to say—tells me more than he should, probably—but *you* seem to see all these *other* things, like camels blocking Cadillacs and impeding American statecraft, or women batting their eyelashes at Foster—they do like him, you know, although he doesn't really realize it." On another occasion, when she heard about Churchill's description of her husband as "the only bull I know who carries his china closet with him," she said, with a small smile, "Sir Winston has his own china shop, but his cups are always filled . . . with spirit . . . and, I suppose, it is just too heavy for him to carry around. Of course, Foster admires him greatly. We *all* do."

She loved my story about the Scotland Yard Inspector who had told me that Churchill's successor, Anthony Eden, liked to joke about "dull, duller, Dulles," but, my Yard friend had added his own footnote by telling me that I shouldn't take it "too personal," coming, as it did, from a "fopwash" like Eden. Indeed, she liked that story so much that she told Dulles about it and he asked me if "fopwash" could be translated into French and German. I told him

that I was not at all sure that it could be translated into *English.*

I believe that Dulles wanted a French translation of "fopwash" so that he could pass it on to General de Gaulle, who, he said, had described Churchill to him as being like aging brandy—"fine if taken in small doses." Secretary and Mrs. Dulles were both pleased when I told them that a French policeman had said that de Gaulle described Dulles as *"formidable!"* Janet Dulles rolled *formidable* around on her tongue with relish and a glint in her eyes, adding, "General de Gaulle is wise, and he doesn't know the half of it . . . at least," she added, more seriously, "I don't think that he does . . . that is, of course, there is espionage, isn't there? . . . intelligence services . . . Good heavens! They do keep files on Foster, don't they? Dossiers? Of course they do. Allen *told* me they did."

I had long suspected that Janet Dulles' view of espionage was like something out of an E. Phillips Oppenheim novel, despite the fact—or maybe because of the fact—that her brother-in-law was Director of Central Intelligence. I say "maybe" because Allen Dulles himself frequently acted as if he was walking through the middle of an old and highly romantic spy story. But I was never quite sure about her views until I heard her answer to my question, "Mrs. Dulles, are you asking me about some file the French may have on the Secretary?"

"Oh, Lou," she said, "you don't have to be polite with me. Of course the French—particularly the French, much as I love them—have a dossier on Foster. They have them on all *kinds* of people. It does seem, well, eerie though that they have Foster in there with all those, uh, munitions makers and jewel thieves and headwaiters—just think of Foster and all those headwaiters—and people who ride the Orient Express and, oh, interior decorators from San Francisco and hairdressers from Nice and, well, people like that . . . people with a . . . role, in things, in a manner of speaking."

"Mrs. Dulles," I responded, "I doubt that they have the Secretary in there with jewel thieves, and headwaiters, and interior decorators from San Francisco."

"Munitions makers?" she asked.

"Yes, well, some munitions makers, I suppose," I said, wondering which part of the century we were in, adding, "Of course, some munitions makers become diplomats, statesmen . . ."

"Merchants of Death," she said quickly, in a huff, "may move the world, but they are *not* statesmen."

"Merchants of Death," I said, savoring the phrase. "Sounds sort of old-fashioned."

"I may be old-fashioned," she said sharply, "but I don't know a better way to describe munitions makers than as Merchants of Death. It is precise and it is accurate."

"Yes," I said, "but, nowadays, we're coming up with all sorts of fancy names and splitting atoms and breaking sound barriers . . ."

She interrupted me. "If you are going through 'sound barriers' to kill . . . well, death is death."

"Yes, ma'am, but . . ."

"Lou," she interrupted again, with feeling, "don't be concerned. I certainly agree with Foster that we have to be ready to fight if we are to avoid another war, but, well, I like accuracy, and Merchants of Death *is* accurate."

"What about headwaiters?"

"Headwaiters can be most important."

"Ma'am?"

"Lou, I'm indulging myself somewhat. Foster would not find all this very funny."

"I guess he wouldn't," I agreed, "but he certainly likes accuracy."

She thought about that for a minute. Then, "Yes, Foster

likes accuracy, but he also says that sometimes it is best to keep things unclear."

"Well, we are in a different time."

"Of course," she agreed. "'Sound barriers.' Munitions makers today are not called Merchants of Death. They are called industrial giants. In the twenties we called them what they were—munitions makers and Merchants of Death. Mysterious people riding around in dark yachts on the Riviera. Now, they all sit around in offices."

"I see," I said.

"No, Lou, you don't, really. You can't. You're not old enough."

Janet Dulles was quite a lady.

As to "fopwash," Dulles did manage, I think, to translate it for de Gaulle. I am also pretty sure that he managed, somehow, to convey its meaning to Konrad Adenauer. He asked me to repeat the story in Bonn, just before a meeting with the old Chancellor. Dulles enjoyed Adenauer's company and felt close to him. Indeed, it was on that particular Bonn visit that I heard West German protocol chief Von Braun (the rocket expert's brother) remark, "We Germans do not know whether Foster Dulles likes *us* or not, but we *know* that he loves our Adenauer."

I don't know whether or not Dulles "loved" Adenauer, but he certainly *did* like and admire the Chancellor. They were genuinely close. So close, in fact, that a man I later discovered to be a Soviet agent questioned me at length one night as to the possibility that they might be related.

It was at a carnival party in Bonn where everybody, including the Soviet agent, was German but me. Two German detectives had promised to show me "things the Americans never see," namely, a big, all-German beer bust. When we first entered the enormous hall, I felt very much alone. Singing Germans filled the place. They were spilling out the door. The man who turned out to be a

Soviet agent (he was paid by an East German intelligence service operated by the KGB) was introduced to me as a "refugee from the East." My friends with the West German police were, at that time, also paying him a small retainer, thinking that they had doubled him back on the Soviets. He looked drunk, but it was hard to be sure. His face reminded me of a wrinkled elbow, but his body showed signs of care and training—all meat and springs. The first thing he did was spill a mug of beer on me. Then, in a seemingly drunken fashion, he began muttering outrageous things like, "Foster, Allen, and Konrad Dulles—Hah! The Chancellor is the third brother, no? Huh? No?"

To my denials, he would retort, "Then where is the *real* Konrad Adenauer—in one of Allen Dulles' 'safe' places?"

When I showed anger, he bored in with, "You do not even *know* when the substitution was made, do you?" and jumped right back to the third man theme—"Ah hah!!!" he shouted. "So, there *are* three Dulles brothers—Foster, Allen, and Konrad."

It went on and on. I started laughing. The whole idea of Konrad Dulles got past my sense of reason and into my sense of humor. Konrad Dulles, Chancellor of the Federal Republic of Germany. Marvelous. But, my laughter brought on a ferocious temper tantrum in the "East" German, so ferocious and so loud that the police escorted him out of the building.

At the time, I dismissed the man from my mind as a screwed-up, triple-agent drunk, although I did mention the incident to an FBI friend, whose reaction was, "Even though the CIA is run by your boss's brother, they just aren't good enough to pull something like *that* off. Adenauer is undoubtedly Adenauer." Later, I was told by the Germans that the man, although playing both sides, had never really given up his allegiance to the Soviets and

that he had "somehow" disappeared "into the East."

I told Dulles about the "third Dulles brother" as a joke, thinking that it would give him a laugh. He didn't crack a smile. Instead, he said, somewhat enigmatically, "The real thing is always much superior to the illusion."

My response was a soft, startled, "Sir?"

Dulles' forefinger was running up and down his nose. He sounded as though he was reading his words. "Our intelligence operations did not just start with the OSS and the CIA. My uncle, Robert Lansing—Woodrow Wilson's Secretary of State—set up an intelligence operation in the State Department during the first World War—*before* America got in—and I remember him talking about substituting one man in a position of power for another man in a position of power."

I was not sure what Dulles was telling me, but it was not a joke. However, still in a light vein, I responded with, "I bet when the only way the whole United States government could get to Woodrow Wilson was through his wife, or his doctor, your uncle would have *liked* to put in a new one—a whole new Woodrow Wilson."

Dulles' forehead wrinkled. His eyes crinkled. His mouth sloped downward on both sides, instead of just one. He said, "Yes, well, that *was* a difficult time. Difficult. Wilson was a great man, but, my uncle Lansing had a . . . difficult . . . another Wilson? . . . tempting, tempting, but, you see . . . it was difficult . . . hmmmmm."

He gave me the feeling that he was defending his uncle, but why? I asked, "Are you saying that a substitute, a new, or 'dummy' Wilson was considered, or tried, or . . . ?"

Dulles' face gave one of its heavier twitches. "No, no, no. That is, well, certainly it might have been *considered*. People today can't grasp how difficult that situation was—the President sick behind closed doors—but . . .

substitution . . . it wouldn't, probably, for one thing, have worked . . . that is, Allen is better at this sort of thing than I am, but, what you must understand is that it was a terrible time and some of the people in government were desperate . . . desperate . . . seeing plots on Mrs. Wilson's part, his physician, Grayson, others. But, I revered Wilson. We all did. At Princeton . . . afterward . . ." His voice faded, but he continued. "We were all so idealistic then, but, ideals with no foundation in truth are . . . are, well, dangerous, and Wilson . . . Wilson didn't always know how to combine thought and action and that was part of my uncle Lansing's problem, but the real thing was access. They just plain could not get to him! My uncle even made a move to have the Vice-President take over the job, or, the cabinet—there were those who accused him of attempting a coup d'état (ha!)—and, certainly, a number of things were tried, but, well . . ." His voice wandered off.

I *had* to ask the question. "You are saying, Mr. Secretary, that your uncle, Secretary of State Robert Lansing, thought of trying to substitute somebody for President Wilson?"

"No," he replied, "that is not what I said."

"But, it *was* considered?"

The skin on his face shook as he responded, "It might . . . have been . . . considered."

"Actually considered, Mr. Secretary?"

"It was a difficult time."

I didn't know whether I was hearing some kind of hidden history or dreaming. I said, "But Konrad Adenauer is not your brother."

Dulles twitched a smile. "That's a marvelous story."

"Maybe it wouldn't do any harm if the Soviets believed he *was* your brother."

"Maybe not," he said. "One minute they're saying he is

my tool, and the next minute they're saying I'm *his* tool, so . . ."

"So, if you were brothers, it would at least explain it all to them."

"Yes," he chuckled. "That's good. But, it's incredible, isn't it, how far people will go in crazy theories like that?"

"Well, if your uncle thought about substituting somebody for Woodrow Wilson . . . ?"

"I didn't say that, Lou," he laughed. "I didn't say that. Did I?"

As with so many of our conversations, that one was interrupted by the necessity for Dulles to conduct United States foreign policy. It receded to the back of my mind until a stop in Bonn on Dulles' last trip to Europe, in January 1959. It was not generally known at the time that he was dying of cancer, but Adenauer pulled me aside and, giving me that stern Mount Rushmore look, asked through an interpreter, "Tell me, and you would know, what is the truth about my friend Dulles' health? I have this feeling that I will not see him again."

He had caught me unawares, and before I could think I blurted out, "Mr. Dulles is sick, very sick." Then I caught myself and added, "But, of course you will see him again. He is planning to live a long time."

The old Chancellor just stared at me, sadness coming through the granite of his normally fixed expression. Finally, he said, "We are brothers, you know. Brothers."

It gave me a shiver as my mind flashed back to the carnival party. A cold shiver.

Dulles and I did not discuss the "Konrad Dulles" story again, but we did talk about the relationship between his uncle, Robert Lansing, and Woodrow Wilson. He told me, "They said that the Secretary of State—my uncle Lansing—tried to make the President, Woodrow Wilson, a puppet. History does have a way of repeating itself. Nowadays, I am described as turning Eisenhower into a puppet. It's nonsense. If anything, it's the other way around."

"You are the President's puppet?"

"Well, no, but President Eisenhower is certainly the one who pulls the strings—not me."

"He sure listens to you," I said.

"He may *listen* to me, but I follow *his* instructions. He is the President. Not me. That's the kind of thing you don't want to forget."

"I just meant you have influence."

"Oh, yes, I have influence. But, not only is he the President, but people *like* him . . . something I don't have."

"You described yourself to Dave Waters [his media adviser] as a cold fish."

"I am. At least people think I am. As a practical matter, I guess that's what counts—what people think they see, rather than what is actually there. Anyway, I know that in some ways I *am* a cold fish, and that I'm afraid is that."

"I don't think so."

"You're prejudiced." He smiled.

"I am," I agreed.

"Well," he said, thoughtfully, working his finger along the side of his nose, "the President is the President, and *he* is more like a warm elk, and sometimes it's all I can do to keep him on the track—get him to thinking about the Soviets instead of underarm deodorants and UFOs."

I was incredulous. "The President believes in UFOs?"

"Yes. I told him he better think about Soviet bombers."

"But, UFOs! And underarm deodorants! Why, that's marvelous. I mean, Wiley Buchanan [his Chief of Protocol] was talking about a special trade agreement that would allow him and me to sell them to the Soviet Union, but . . ."

Dulles roared. "Sell underarm deodorants to the Soviet

Union? *That* is a good one. I'll have to tell President Eisenhower about it. But what he wanted me to do was talk to Bernie Baruch about the investment prospects."

I couldn't believe it. "President Eisenhower is interested in the investment prospects in underarm deodorants?"

"Yes."

"Is he serious?"

"Well, he was laughing, and, there were other things, but, yes . . ."

"I guess Baruch would know," I said.

"The important thing is the President believes that Bernie would know." Dulles chuckled.

"About underarm deodorants?"

"Well, not about the chemical properties."

"The investment prospects, the money to be made."

"Yes," Dulles clucked.

"Amazing."

"Did Wiley really propose selling underarm deodorants to the Soviets?"

"Yes, sir."

"Was he serious?" Dulles asked, looking as if it couldn't possibly be serious.

"At first, I didn't think so. You know Wiley's crazy sense of humor."

"Yes. Irreverant. But, marvelous."

"Exactly."

Thoughtfully, he said, "Maybe I should suggest that he, Wiley, propose it to the President."

"You mean have the President replace me as Wiley Buchanan's underarm deodorant partner?"

"That's good."

This was crazy, I thought. I said, "I met Baruch."

"I know you did—you were with *me* at the time."

"I know I was," I agreed. "I met his masseuse, too."

"Is *that* what she was?" Dulles twinkled.

"Yes, sir. You saw her."

"Oh, yes. I saw her. Big, strapping woman. I wondered . . ."

"About the massage?" I asked.

"Yes," he grinned. "About the massage." He was laughing hard, now. "Actually, doesn't he call her his 'companion'?"

"That's right. She told me that having alcohol rubbed into your pores was much better than drinking it."

"Good Lord!" His whole upper body twitched. "She actually *told* you that?"

"Yes, sir. Do you think there's an underarm deodorant connection, here?"

"I don't know." He grinned. "It does remind me of a story. Years ago, a group of us were with Baruch and, out of a clear blue sky, he asked us, 'Do I smell different?' We wondered what he'd been drinking until he continued with, 'Aren't we Jews supposed to smell different, and that's why we're not wanted in certain places, certain clubs? Isn't that why we're 'advisers' to kings, but rarely kings?' That's what he said. And, then he said, 'Maybe we should all wear perfume. Disraeli wore perfume and *he* became more than an adviser—he became Prime Minister of England. Most of us just become advisers.'" Dulles paused, thinking, and continued, "Baruch doesn't, as a rule, make much of being Jewish . . . slights, discrimination . . . and, when he does, he has this marvelous sense of fun . . . mockery . . . but, perfume, underarm deodorants." His voice drifted away, and then came back with, "But you and Wiley Buchanan in business selling underarm deodorants to the Soviets! Extraordinary. You know, Wiley told me once that the Saudi Arabians didn't drink—Islam and such—and I told him that I had *seen* some of them drink, and he said, well, they didn't drink in Washington because Washington was sacred. Can you imagine that? I never heard anybody describe Washington as sacred."

I hadn't either. I said, "I think Wiley was just trying to resolve some protocol difficulties during a Saudi visit."

Assuming his best preacher-Dulles look, Dulles retorted, "Yes, well, I understand some of the Saudis even smoke hashish."

"Dope?" I asked, shocked not by what he had said, but that he had said it.

"Is that what you call it?"

"That's what we used to call it in my jazz musician days."

"When you were a jazz musician?"

"When I was sixteen, seventeen years old," I responded, not really wanting to get into it.

"Did you *try* this dope?" he asked, looking genuinely interested.

"Not hashish."

"Something else?"

"Not since."

Bemused, "Lou, you really are remarkable, that is, here you are, my security officer . . ."

"Yes, sir, well, when you're around jazz musicians you are generally around dope, drugs."

"Jazz musicians. Hmmmmmmmmm. But they don't smoke hashish?"

"Mr. Secretary, I didn't say that."

"No, you didn't," he agreed. "But, it's interesting. Some of Allen's people are experimenting with what you probably call dope—strange drugs. I don't know just what I think of that."

"I'm sure the Soviets are experimenting with all kinds of drugs."

"That's what Allen says."

"Your brother should know," I said, adding, "When Wiley Buchanan heard that Joe McCarthy was saying that your brother and the CIA were soft on Communism, he said, 'Saying Allen Dulles is soft on Communism is like saying Texas oilmen want to get rid of the depletion allowance.'"

"Wiley's a man of very pronounced views," Dulles smiled, "and, although I agree with a lot of those views, I did ask him once if having strong views didn't hinder him in his job as Chief of Protocol; that is, wouldn't it be better for a Chief of Protocol to have, well, *no* views. Wiley said that people who held *no* views were generally dead and that although some of the world's protocol chiefs might *seem* dead, most of them were still alive."

"Most of them?"

"That's what he said."

"So, according to Wiley, *some* of the world's protocol chiefs are dead, even though they still hold office."

"Yes, well, of course, Wiley also thinks Joe Kennedy's going to make Jack Kennedy president."

"And you don't think so?" I asked.

"Oh, yes, it could happen," he replied. "Joe is determined, and Jack is an attractive young man. And . . . Wiley. Wiley is just plain remarkable, sometimes. He'll tell you things you don't want to hear and convince you that you do want to hear them, and, well, he radiates energy and that car of his—what is it?"

"I think it's a Bentley."

"That's it," he agreed. "A Bentley, and when he gets out of it in front of Blair House with those two lovely little girls of his . . ."

"Dede and Bonnie."

"Yes, and, well, he looks like a pasha."

"That's the American way." I laughed.

"What do you mean by that?" he asked seriously.

"Every man has a right to look like a pasha."

"Harumph!" he snorted. "Nobody would ever mistake *me* for a pasha."

"I think some people have."

"Impossible."

"Well," I said, "Wiley calls you 'boss,' so if he's a pasha, that makes you the Supreme Pasha."

"This is nonsense, but I like Wiley, and Janet says his wife, Ruth, is the 'real thing.'"

"The real thing?"

"The real thing!" he said, with finality.

Ironically, years later, Wiley Buchanan's nephew, Doug Inglish, who loved him dearly and was close to him, told me that Wiley admired Dulles because he felt that the Secretary was "the real thing." Whatever the case, Dulles enjoyed Wiley's irreverent remarks on people like Jack Kennedy, but the Secretary really surprised me when he responded to my observation that Kennedy would appeal to the "restless, the young" with, "Bet you didn't know I used to just go out and riot when I was a student in Paris."

"Mr. Secretary," I responded, "that's the kind of thing people might well suspect of John Kennedy, but *not* John Foster Dulles."

"Jack Kennedy's too controlled for that sort of thing," Dulles said shortly, adding, "He looks rumpled, but he'd never riot. Controlled rumpledness."

"Everything by the numbers."

"In a manner of speaking."

"Yes, sir, but, *you* . . . *rioting* . . . and in Paris, too!"

"What better place than Paris for a good riot?" he asked smugly.

"Fine place," I responded.

"Sure. I'd just stuff my hat full of paper—those police clubs can hurt—and go out and riot."

"Amazing."

"In retrospect it is. We'd riot all over the place, over all sorts of things. Yes, and," he said thoughtfully, "here I am trying to keep the peace of the whole world."

"And, now," I said, "when you go to Paris, you meet with Charles de Gaulle. What do you think General de Gaulle would think if he knew you used to riot in Paris?"

"You've met de Gaulle."

"I shook his hand."

"Well?"

"Sir?"

His exasperation was showing. "If you've *seen* him, you should *know* what he'd think."

"I would think that if you had rioted in London, that would not impress him. He'd just say the British deserved it, and you were showing your good sense. But, the fact that you rioted in Paris, like a good *French* student—*that* would impress him."

Dulles nodded his approval. "Good thinking."

"Since he's come back to power, de Gaulle has certainly gotten the French bureaucrats jumping."

"My Lord, yes," Dulles agreed. "I asked one of their Foreign Office people about a paper and he said that the General would have it in his hands and read it at seven that evening. When I asked 'No later than seven?' this fella said, 'No earlier either, because the General said that he wished to see the paper *at* seven!' Amazing. Not after seven! Not before seven! *At* seven. He's got them all not only working, but constantly checking their clocks and watches."

"The Clock Mystique—good title for a study of this 'new' French diplomacy."

Dulles cluck-clucked some laughter, saying, "You're just full of original thoughts here."

"Yes, sir. You really hit it off with de Gaulle, didn't you?"

"I think so. President Eisenhower told me that too many people make the mistake of approaching de Gaulle like a lion tamer approaching a lion, instead of using a snake charmer's approach."

"You mean President Eisenhower told you to treat de Gaulle like a snake?"

"No, no," Dulles demurred. "*Charm* him like a snake. There's a difference."

"Even so, Mr. Secretary, aren't you saying that President Eisenhower sees General de Gaulle as some kind of snake?"

"Of course not. Churchill might see him that way. Churchill loves to call people snakes and buzzards and things like that. But President Eisenhower *knows* General de Gaulle, and General de Gaulle spoke to me of his high regard for the President and myself. Now, that doesn't mean you don't have to deal with the General gingerly. His ego is enormous, and you just have to recognize that right from the beginning."

"He does have an ego," I agreed, "but if he didn't, he would have probably ended up an obscure French tank officer without any tanks, and maybe without any France."

"True," Dulles agreed. "I admire him. We get along."

"You *charmed* him, Mr. Secretary."

"Hah!" he barked. "From what you told me, it's *you* who's the charmer."

"Sir?" I questioned. Then, I remembered, saying, softly, "Ahhh, the Lady of the Lake." I had forgotten that I had told him of her and her reappearance.

8

The Lady of the Lake

When I got back to Washington after the Geneva summit, I found myself fighting a series of vicious headaches. Advice on how to handle them was plentiful. The best came from a bartender who, himself, suffered from chronic mental arthritis. In spite of this, or, perhaps because of it, he had become a valued counselor to many of America's foreign service personnel. His place of business was near the State Department, but not too near. It was an easy walk, but you still had the sense of being in hiding when you got there. The atmosphere was perfect—crummy enough to add to your sense of security, but not so crummy that you could feel the bugs coming up your legs. In any case, when I took my problem to him, he said, in effect, "Ride right through the middle of that pain, face it, and stick your finger up its ass."

Good advice. Even so, it really gave me only a psychological lift. The pain persisted. I needed more than words.

A public health nurse at the State Department told me that I was "undoubtedly" suffering from "delayed airplane shock." When I asked her what delayed airplane shock was, she said, "You fly too much." That did not help. I got desperate. Indeed, I got so desperate that one winter morning I drove over to Ocean City, Maryland—close to 200 miles. The tide started out as I arrived. I could feel the great Atlantic ocean inhaling. My mind seemed to go with it. I wondered what was happening? The season was long over, and the boardwalk was nearly empty.

A woman handed me a tin of aspirin and disappeared. At first I couldn't remember where I had seen her before. Then, I remembered. The Lady of the Lake. I opened the tin and found two aspirins. Or, were they aspirins? Whatever they were, my head was killing me.

I walked into a restaurant, got a glass of water, and took the two pills. My headache cleared and did not return with such malignant force until I found it necessary to stop drinking, over fifteen years later.

Returning to Washington from Ocean City, I wondered if I had imagined the whole thing. I *still* wonder. But it was a busy time, and, although I did not come up with an answer, I soon forgot the question. Forgot it, that is, until one night some months later, when I found myself in a Saigon bar frequented by aging French Foreign Legionnaires and renegade intelligence operatives. I was sitting at a table rather than at the bar because on a previous visit a large rat had run right down the bar in front of me. It was an ugly place, in a building that might have been transported from some French flea market and left to sweat—a bruise on Saigon's still attractive (1956) landscape. I was sharing the mourner's breakfast—gin and juice—with a woman from our embassy who had told me that she was in "cultural affairs." That was her story. However, I had been told in great secrecy by a security colleague that she worked for military intelligence. And the Vietnamese police said flat out that she worked for the CIA's Saigon station. I chose to go along with the cultural affairs cover and set out to impress her with stories of my meetings with Ezra Pound and T. S. Eliot when I was a poetry-writing student at Washington's George Washington University. We were discussing something about slogans serving as the soul of America, except, of course, there *was* jazz, and cowboy art, and . . . in walked a woman who looked just like the Lady of the Lake. She came right over to our table and said, "Hello."

I stood up and mumbled through a barely swallowed gulp of gin, "Won't you sit down?"

Before she could answer, another rat leaped off the bar and came hurtling through the air like a guided missile aimed straight at us. I ducked and found myself clutching the Lady of the Lake and being clutched by my companion from "cultural affairs."

The Lady of the Lake said, "It's so good to see you," as we struggled back into our chairs.

"You *are* a charmer!" the lady from "cultural affairs" whispered in my ear, biting it before adding, "She looks like Marilyn Monroe."

"Who works for who, here?" I said to both women as they ignored me, sizing each other up. The Lady of the Lake *did* look like Marilyn Monroe. I hadn't noticed it before. I asked her, "Are you Marilyn Monroe?"

"No, but, we—she and I—are close," she replied.

"Marilyn Monroe works for the CIA?" I asked, jokingly. The reply was serious. "No, but she would like to."

My face felt like a question mark. "Marilyn Monroe would *like* to work for the CIA?"

"Yes," she smirked.

"My God!" I said, beginning to feel the booze—indeed, feeling more booze than I had consumed. Thought vanished, replaced by nothing. I came to in what appeared to be a barracks in a rice paddy. In actual fact, it was where the Embassy's Marine guards were quartered at the time—a barracks in a rice paddy. A sergeant of my acquaintance shook me awake, saying, "We thought you were dead."

"Are you sure that I'm *not* dead?" I asked.

"You *seem* alive," the Marine responded.

"I don't know."

"You better decide."

"Whether I'm dead or not?"

"Right!"

I had a mental flash of the face of John Foster Dulles. His scowl was sagging. I got up and got going. A State Department security colleague and the Saigon police were, I knew, with Dulles, but I wanted to reach him ahead of the inevitable rumor of my demise.

I got to our Saigon Embassy residence just in time to spot a boy in short pants (not Bermuda shorts, or gym shorts, or jogging shorts, but *short pants*) wandering around the grounds with a .22 rifle. He didn't look Vietnamese. He didn't look French. He didn't look American. He almost didn't look at all, but, there he was, waving a .22 rifle around while Dulles appeared to be posing, full figure, in a French window. I shouted at the boy. He started to run. I tackled him and we wrestled until we found ourselves looking up into the beaming face of U.S. Ambassador to Saigon G. Frederick Reinhardt, from Berkeley, California, a fine diplomat and outstanding drinker. I was to come to know Reinhardt well, but, at that juncture, I didn't know him at all. He was saying, in a sort of gutteral lisp, "I say, now, you two, there, you're both trying to achieve the same thing—security. So, stop trying to kill one another and get after those boys with the plastique."

I got up, pointing at the kid, and asking, "Who in the hell is he?"

"The Eurasian cook's son—father unknown," Reinhardt replied, with a big, big smile.

At that moment, I believe that I wanted to forget the kid and slug the Honorable G. Frederick Reinhardt, little suspecting that, just two years later, Reinhardt and I would be involved together—indeed, we were the principal players—in what came to be known as The Great John Foster Dulles Caviar Rescue Mission. We were in Ankara, Turkey, having just been in Tehran, Iran, where all gifts of caviar to the Secretary and others in the party, as well as caviar purchases, were handled, one way or another, by an agent of the Shah. Outside of the Soviet Union, Iran was *the* place for caviar, and Dulles shared with Reinhardt, who had replaced Douglas MacArthur II as State Department Counselor, a love for if not an addiction to good caviar. The Shah's agent had assured us that prior to our departure for Ankara all of the accumulated caviar had been delivered to our aircraft's hold. Our Air Force crew assured me that this was so. But, in Ankara, first Dulles, and then Reinhardt, started to worry about it. I assured them that it was plenty cold enough to keep the caviar at the proper temperature in the parked aircraft's hold, but Reinhardt, after consultations with Dulles, decided that it was necessary for us to go out to the aircraft, which was at an airport well outside of town, and make sure the caviar was there. "The Secretary," he said to me, "is worried about it, and, when it comes to caviar, *I* do not trust the Shah."

I couldn't resist asking, "Is caviar the only area where you don't trust the Shah?"

"Caviar is symbolic."

"Symbolic?"

"Of Iranian nationalism."

"What do you mean by that?"

"They'll use it against you."

"Caviar?"

"Yes," Reinhardt said decisively, "and anybody who will use caviar against you is beneath . . . well, you figure it out."

"You mean," I asked, "that the Shah of Iran would use caviar against John Foster Dulles?"

"Give him a chance and he will," Reinhardt pronounced. "You've got to remember that in spite of what the Russians say, the Persians practically invented caviar."

"Right, but you've got me worried, that is, what could they, the Shah and his men, do to use it, caviar, *against* Dulles?"

Reinhardt's head went back. Way, way back. His face was pointing skyward, but his eyes were looking down between puffy cheeks at me, as he replied, "Just suppose, Lou, that we get out to the plane and find the hold filled, not with caviar, but, with . . . say, herring. Think about it. Herring. Can you imagine the Secretary's reaction? I shudder to speculate on how it might affect his frame of mind. It might affect our whole negotiating position here at this conference. Why, it could, even, mean war."

"War?" I asked, not believing my ears. "Over herrings replacing caviar? Aren't you overstating this?"

"Wars have been started over less," Reinhardt said, looking wise and adding, "and, always remember, the frame of mind of the mighty is a delicate matter."

When I agreed that that was certainly so, he said, "Yes, and we'd better drink on it."

Before we had the drink, we went out to the aircraft. It was dark, and we arrived in a Turkish Army jeep with a lieutenant waving a flashlight crazily in the direction of our parked plane. We were told that the lieutenant, with his flashlight, was like our flag of truce—without him we would be shot by Turkish guards, most of whom were, according to Turkish officials, "simple country boys."

It was a long, bumpy ride out over that darkened airstrip, with the lieutenant's flashlight waving, and the barely discernible figures of the guards around the aircraft motionless and silent in the dark distance. The lieutenant was jumpy. You could feel his nerves, smell them coming out through his pores. I wondered how the press would play it if the Department of State's Counselor and John Foster Dulles' bodyguard got shot while trying to check a load of caviar because the Counselor thought that the Shah of Iran might set out to incite war, and worse, by replacing the caviar with herring. The story of the century, I thought, as one of the guards challenged us. I couldn't understand the words, but it was clearly a challenge, and he, apparently, was not going to shoot first. A surge of hope went through me. It looked as though we were going to make it to the plane alive. The lieutenant kept shouting at them, and the words must have been right because they let us get to the plane. The caviar was okay. No herring. Reinhardt did a little dance right there on that dark, silent airstrip. He said he'd learned it in Budapest in 1925. One of the Turkish soldiers laughed, dropped his rifle, and started his own dance. The lieutenant signaled another jeep with his flashlight. A high-pitched, female voice came at us out of the dark. A shot went off in the distance. Bombs had already blown out the back of the nearby American Embassy information section, and I thought we were under attack. When I heard a second shot, I hit the ground, but Reinhardt kept right on dancing, saying it must be the Shah "coming for his caviar." The Turkish soldiers were all dancing and waving flashlights. A strange scene. Surrealistic.

When we got back into Ankara, I thought Dulles would

pin medals on us when he learned that the caviar was in good shape. Reinhardt told me later, on the plane leaving Turkey (over a tin of caviar) that the airport exercise had made us "blood brothers." However, he didn't even look friendly in that Saigon Embassy yard. But I did get my first demonstration of his rather formidable diplomatic technique, when he sternly commended me for "stopping" the kid, and sternly commended the kid for "stopping" me.

I got the rifle away from the kid by telling him that if he gave it to me, I would show him how to clean it. He liked that, and followed me inside where Dulles said, "Lou, that was one of your more amazing performances."

Later, during the same Saigon visit, I told Dulles, without going into all the details, about the Lady of the Lake and said, "This woman who keeps popping up around the world—she may be KGB, or . . . some other intelligence service close to the KGB—but I just saw her here in Saigon and she tells me Marilyn Monroe wants to work for the CIA."

I was not unaccustomed to the Dulles look of disbelief, but I was unprepared for his opinion that "that sounds like something William F. Buckley would come up with."

"Do you read William F. Buckley, Jr.?" I asked.

"I am familiar with him," he replied.

"I see," I said, not seeing at all. "But, why would William F. Buckley, Jr., say that Marilyn Monroe wanted to work for the CIA?"

"Well," Dulles responded impatiently, "Buckley has a sense of humor that says things."

"I'm not sure what we are saying, here, Mr. Secretary," I said.

"Neither am I," Dulles responded. "But, it's interesting. I'll mention it to Allen."

"Marilyn Monroe?"

"Yes."

"Maybe she's already working for your brother."

"It's possible," Dulles said with a smile, adding, "But, if she is, Allen might not tell me, although he does like to brag."

"I've heard him." I laughed.

"This whole business of the woman in your hotel room in Geneva—have you talked with any of Allen's people about it?"

"Informally," I said, thinking of a friend who worked for the Agency who thought that I must be having hallucinations.

"What do you mean by 'informally'?" Dulles asked.

"I discussed it with a friend in the CIA," I replied, hesitating to mention hallucinations, but adding that "he didn't seem to take it too seriously."

"I see," Dulles said. "Strange business."

It was a strange business. I began to wonder and worry about myself. I couldn't sleep. I was drinking too much. I found myself pacing the floor in the small hours. The night snakes were slithering down from the trees of my subconsciousness, and I was sometimes terrified. But I couldn't get a handle on it. I knew that the KGB was experimenting with and using what we now call hallucinogens for various purposes. So were other intelligence services, including the CIA. One of my security colleagues became convinced that somebody had slipped me something. "Maybe a joke," he said, "like when you lost your driver in Geneva."

"You mean," I asked him, "that I'm imagining all this Lady of the Lake business?"

"Well," he said, "maybe the woman really was in your room in Geneva and maybe she took your delegation list as a little 'lesson' because she knew you had taken theirs, and—think about it—she was alone in your room before you got there, wasn't she?"

"Yes," I replied, "she was there, alone, when I got there."

"Did you check your toothpaste after she left?" he asked.

"Toothpaste?"

"Right."

"I never thought of it."

"Maybe you should have."

This was too much. I dismissed the whole business from my mind until I thought that I saw her again in the Fiji Islands in an old hotel I dubbed the Maugham-Hilton. It happened while I was sitting at the hotel's massive bar drinking straight gin and listening to the whine of high-pitched boredom punctuated by the flap, flap, flap, of the two-slat fan over my head and the drip, drip, drip of the sweating walls. So many walls in that part of the world seemed to sweat, and I thought about it for awhile. When I asked the moist, dead-faced man in the dirty white suit and Panama hat sitting next to me the time, he turned wet eyes on me and coughed the question, "Young man, just what difference does it make?" Contempt was etched into his face's many glistening creases. I told him that I *needed* the time. He ignored me.

I did need the time. After Dulles and I had visited some banana boats anchored off a mini-jungle, I had left him safely surrounded by British-trained police in the American Consulate-General drinking that Australian beer that hits you like alcohol injected straight to the heart (a constable told me that it had been specially marked for export to the Fijis). Now, in the bar, my watch had stopped, and our plane was due to leave shortly.

The bartender's contempt was not so blatant as that of the man in the Panama hat, but he did give me that "visitor from another planet" look when I told him how much I would appreciate it if he could somehow determine the time for me. Then he spit. His spit dropped slowly to the floor. It had been a gentle spit, carrying with it the failure that permeated the whole sweating room— all the lost opportunities that had found their way to bottles in that seedy place. I could feel it, and I knew that my fellow drinkers *wanted* me to feel it. There I was surrounded by the world's ultimate misfits all wrapped in dirty white suits, with their lower extremities guarded by tennis shoes over bare feet. It was grotesque. Then I saw her, in a straw hat and a clean white dress, looking at her watch. I started toward her, and she went through the swinging doors. I followed her into the street, but she had disappeared once again.

I was in the street. A man in a dirty white suit handed me a bottle of that powerful Australian beer, and, I stood there, in the street, drinking Australian beer and suddenly remembering that Dulles had wanted to go swimming before our plane took off. I pounded my forehead with my fist, took another slug of Australian beer, and ran.

We did go swimming—that is, *he* went swimming, and I stood in the jungle with a white police inspector and a black "bobby." The black man, after watching Dulles in swimming trunks for a few minutes, watched his inspector wander off and said to me, "Meestair Doolays, he is very white. Very, very white."

"Yes," I agreed, "he is."

"Some of you whites are whiter than others," he went on.

"That," I agreed, "is undoubtedly true."

He smiled. "You whites see us blacks as having many shades of black, brown, and so forth, in our color, but most of you do not know that *we* see *you* as having many shades of white. Many shades. It does help us to tell you apart."

"How would you grade *my* color?" I asked.

"Medium," he replied, immediately, adding, with a deep, James Earl Jones laugh, "Yes, medium to very good."

His inspector was returning, and I asked, "What about the inspector—what shade of white is he?"

The black policeman turned serious and responded, "I do not think that he would appreciate this conversation, but you, my friend, I will remember."

He was in the crowd, waving, as we took off, and so, indeed, was the Lady of the Lake.

9

Matches, the Bomb, and Henry Kissinger

During that trip that took me into the jungles of Fiji and the wild wetness of the "Maugham-Hilton," I started reading a book by Henry Kissinger, *Nuclear Weapons and Foreign Policy*, a book that has been described as a "seminal work" on nuclear strategy. I finished it in New York's Waldorf Towers during a UN session and handed it to Dulles, who grunted and growled, "Brilliant young man, Kissinger. Brilliant. Probably be Secretary of State someday. But, my heavens, some of these Pentagon people act as if Professor Kissinger invented the incorporating of atomic weapons into foreign policy. If any *individual* did that, why, I did. Actually, the weapons themselves did it—by being there, waiting to be used in war or incorporated into a policy of firmness and peace. It's got to be one or the other—war or a policy." Dulles had that quality the Romans called *gravitas*, a sense of weight and purpose. It

was really showing as he added, "Because, without a policy, you don't know how long those bombs will wait."

"Yes, sir," I agreed, "but Kissinger *is* bright. I gave Bill
Macomber his first book, *A World Restored*."

Dulles obviously hadn't heard of that one, as he asked,
"Kissinger's making atomic strategy and restoring the
world at the same time?"

"*A World Restored* is about the Congress of Vienna," I
responded.

"The balance of power?"

"Yes."

"I see. Yes, there is a connection. Of course, most of
those Harvard people, except, maybe, Bob Bowie—Bowie
introduced me to Kissinger, or, was it Allen?—but, anyway, most of them at Harvard have not as yet faced the
fact of atomic weapons, but, even so, it seems that
Kissinger has. Actually, most of them at that place don't
seem to recognize the fact that *I* am a fact. I suppose I've
always been suspect with Harvard people because I went
to Princeton, and, even worse, George Washington University Law School. First time I applied for a job at Sullivan
and Cromwell, a pretty big law firm even then, but, anyway, I was told that I didn't fit because Princeton was a
'country club' and none of them ever even heard of George
Washington University."

"I know," I said. "I went to George Washington University, too."

"That's right," he laughed. "Between the two of us,
maybe we can put the place on the map. Wonder if Dr.
Kissinger ever heard of George Washington University?"

"It's possible."

"Lou, anything is possible. Well, almost anything. You
know, it took pull—my grandfather—to eventually get me

that job with Sullivan and Cromwell. They didn't think I'd amount to much."

"You ended up the senior partner."

Dulles' laugh went down into that deep bullfrog, as he said, "Fooled 'em, didn't I? Wasn't easy."

"I suppose," I said, trying to be funny, "that if I had gone to, say, even Princeton, which is considerably more socially acceptable than George Washington, I might have ended up a second secretary in, oh, Karachi, or maybe Rome, rather than as your security officer."

"You passed the written examination for the foreign service, didn't you?" he asked, seriously.

"Yes, but the foreign service does not really want former security officers in its midst," I replied, not laughing.

"You worked for *The Washington Post*," he said, apropos of I knew not what.

"In a lowly capacity," I replied.

"Yes," he said, "but, surely, that is a redeeming quality."

"Redeeming quality? *The Washington Post?* Are you serious, Mr. Secretary?"

"Certainly!" he replied, adding, "I wonder if this Kissinger fella could pass the written examination for the Foreign Service?"

"He probably could," I replied, assuming that the author of *Nuclear Weapons and Foreign Policy* might well be equipped to pass the written examination for the United States Foreign Service.

"Yes, he probably could," Dulles agreed, thoughtfully.

"Of course, he undoubtedly sees himself as *making* foreign policy rather than carrying it out as a member of the Foreign Service."

"I'm sure you're right." He laughed. "And I think people—the military, in particular—like Kissinger's book because it gives them a way to think about matters they haven't wanted to think about because, I suppose, they didn't know *how* to think about them."

"You mean it gives them a way to put atomic war into more . . . acceptable . . . terms."

"Exactly," he agreed. "But, it's like bad food—really bad food tastes bad no matter what you put on it."

My mind erupted and my mouth said, "A bomb is a bomb is a bomb."

Dulles cleared his throat, and asked, "Where did you come up with that?"

"Gertrude Stein," I replied.

"I've heard of her. Lesbian, wasn't she?"

"I think so."

He cleared his throat again. "I've known a few lesbians. Brilliant people, by and large. Strange."

"They wouldn't get hired in the State Department."

"No, they wouldn't, if it were known, anyway. Seems unfair, doesn't it? Some really brilliant diplomats have been homosexuals, you know."

He didn't name any names, and I hesitated before trying one. Finally, I said, simply, "Sumner Welles."

"Contrary to what some might think, I was never a great admirer of Welles!" Dulles snorted. "Still . . . tragic business. Dreadful stories. There he was, Undersecretary of State, and . . . those stories."

"About him and his driver," I said.

"Yes," Dulles said sadly.

"He was protected by President Roosevelt. They were neighbors or something, weren't they?"

"Yes, I think so. Something like that. Blackmail is the danger. Has been throughout history. Strange business, anyway. Some of the strangest stories I've ever heard were about Ivar Kreuger, the so-called Swedish Match King, but, the thing is, he had this Swedish massage woman—something like Baruch—and, actually, when he died, the world was littered with his women as well as his debts, but, you see, they say, he, uh, liked men, too."

"Ivar Kreuger?"

"Yes, the Swedish Match King."

"You mean," I asked, "matches as in flames?"

"That's right," he said. "Kreuger put together an extraordinary empire—cornered the world's supply of matches."

"I've never thought of matches as big business."

"Well, think, for a moment, about a world without matches."

"I'm thinking," I said, trying hard to concentrate on matches.

"Before cigarette lighters and all this modern nonsense."

"Right. No cigarette lighters."

He studied me. Then he said, "Good."

"Sir?"

"There is nothing like a good match, is there?"

"No, sir," I agreed, wondering if we were both losing our minds.

Looking satisfied, he said, "Anything but a match ruins a good cigar."

"You don't smoke."

"No more, no. I still like to light a good match now and then, though." There was silence between us for a moment before he added, "You look like you're ready to shoot someone."

"I'm trying to contemplate a world without matches."

He growled as he said, "I spent years trying to unravel the Kreuger situation from a legal standpoint. So many, many people were affected. Debts, losses everywhere. So much money was lost. So many greedy people beating down doors trying to get their investments back. Greed and envy are, in spite of what anyone says, major motivating forces, not only in relations between individuals, but in relations between nations as well. And, if we are ever going to do anything about the war system that governs the world, we will have to do something about greed and envy, and we will have to give nations mechanisms other than war to effect change. We must, somehow, *institutionalize* peace, and, if you are going to institutionalize peace, you've got to have the institutions to do it, and those institutions *must be accepted.*"

Blown back by his vehemence, I mumbled, "From matches to institutionalizing peace . . . a long trip!"

"What?" he asked, sharply.

"Your mind works in amazing ways."

"Well," he responded, even more sharply, "at least it works, which is more than I can say for some of the people I have to deal with."

Still a little startled, I agreed, and asked, "Are the Soviet leaders driven by greed and envy?"

"Envy, certainly," Dulles replied, harshly. "Greed, also, but the greed is more complicated, more . . . subtle. Americans tend to see greed almost solely on an individual basis, not that the Soviet leaders in particular don't enjoy the good things of life. But the Soviet Union is greedy as a nation, just as Tsarist Russia was greedy as a nation. In some instances, of course, greed can be channeled into a positive force."

"Are you thinking of the British Empire?"

"Well, yes, I suppose," he said thoughtfully, "but that was not *always* positive."

"Lots of pomp and circumstance," I responded with a touch of sarcasm.

"Indeed. You know, Janet told me once that I'd fit in the House of Lords, but I told her I was much too common for that and she said what about the Knights of the Garter, but, you know, I've always wondered if they actually wore garters? Do you know if they do?"

"Do I know if the Knights of the Garter actually wear garters?"

"Yes. It's something that has always puzzled me."

"Well," I said, "you could always ask Winston Churchill."

"My Lord, yes," Dulles exclaimed, "that's what *he* is, isn't it?"

"Yes, sir. Not just any old knight, but a Knight of the Garter."

"Extraordinary!" Dulles said, sounding as if he meant it.

"You could ask him if he actually wears one."

"Harumph!" Dulles grumped. "Winston would probably tell me that he wears Sarah Bernhardt's garter."

"Sarah Bernhardt?"

"Yes. Or Greta Garbo."

"Did Greta Garbo wear garters?"

"Harumph."

"Yes, sir."

"I don't know about Greta Garbo," Dulles said, adding with emphasis, "but Sarah Bernhardt certainly did!"

"You have first-hand knowledge?" I asked.

He studied me for a moment, very seriously, before giving a lawyerlike answer. "*That* would be impossible, would it not?"

"She was still alive in the 1920s, wasn't she?" I asked.

Dulles dismissed the subject with a smile, and, "That is a matter for the historians like Dr. Kissinger, isn't it?"

Our conversation was interrupted by the arrival of his brother. They greeted each other and the Director of Central Intelligence turned to me, saying, "Sukarno is now protected by divisions, not just 'elite' platoons."

I remembered Sukarno's arrival at a meeting near Djakarta with his platoons of Sten gun–carrying black-jacketed bodyguards in their helmets and paratroop boots. Before we knew what was happening, they were disappearing behind bushes, climbing trees, and digging foxholes all over the place. Sukarno had tapped me on the shoulder with his swagger stick, given me that big toothy smile, and waved his stick around at his men as if to say, "Look what I've got!" I said to Allen Dulles, "The last time I was in Indonesia I wished Sukarno'd let *us* have some of those 'elite' troops what with the mobs everywhere."

The Director of Central Intelligence chuckled and said, "You should work for me instead of my brother, here, but I wouldn't put you in Djakarta. I'd put you in Germany, or maybe . . . Geneva."

"You've heard about Geneva?" I asked.

"I've heard *many* things about you in Geneva!" the spymaster replied, giving a great Santa Claus laugh before disappearing into another room with his brother, the Secretary of State.

10

In Search of an Enchilada and Related Matters

Let's see, where were we? Oh, yes. Standing in the middle of Mexico City, hoping not to see the Lady of the Lake, while telling Dulles that in spite of enormous logistic support from the Mexican Army, I could not find an enchilada in the capital city of the country that invented the enchilada.

It was the year before Dulles died. The cancer was already on him, but he was functioning as if it wasn't. We were in Mexico City for the inauguration of President López Mateos, and Dulles was not thinking about enchiladas, but he said, "Enchilada? That's border food, isn't it?"

"Where'd you hear *that?*" I asked.

"Lyndon Johnson told me, I think," he replied.

"Texas. Sure. *He'd* know about the border."

Dulles' snort was like a backward sniff, where the smell goes out rather than in. He said, "I had to listen to Lyndon go on and on one time about Mexican food as a, a, er, 'sexual power builder.'"

I wanted to be sure that I had heard correctly. "A sexual *power* builder?" I asked.

"Well, you know how Senator Johnson is," Dulles said, matter-of-factly.

"I know he likes to boast about his alleged sexual power, but I never heard it attributed to—my God!—Mexican food!" I cracked up.

Dulles gave that backward sniff again. "Lyndon said that he uses Mexican food for a laxative, too. Said he learned it from his father—that when his father was constipated, he'd go out, and, according to Lyndon, 'campaign the Mexicans' and they'd feed him a lot of Mexican food—the father, that is—and then, Lyndon said, 'the old man'd clean right out' . . . but, oh yes, *who* in the Mexican Army is seeking your enchilada?"

"There is this captain," I replied, "but part of the problem is that he is actually a lieutenant who has *said* that he is a captain for so long that he now truly *believes* that he is a captain when, in actual fact, he is a lieutenant."

Dulles' eye gave a severe twitch. "How," he asked, "did you acquire this somewhat unusual information?"

"It was explained to me by a colonel whom the Mexican government has got watching us."

"Watching *who*?"

"Us."

"I see," Dulles said. "And this captain who is actually a lieutenant?"

"This captain-lieutenant has apparently involved much of the Mexican Army in the search for my enchilada."

"Preposterous!" Dulles bellowed. "Still, it does seem that you should be able to find an enchilada in the middle of Mexico City. I wonder if López Mateos is aware of the fact that you have the Mexican Army searching for an enchilada?"

Later, when I told Dulles that I had located an entire enchilada dinner, he was relieved, until I added that my quest had ended *not* in a Mexican restaurant, but in the American Embassy canteen. "I wonder what Milton Eisenhower would think of *that?*" he asked finally, referring to a conversation with the President's brother on our flight down. We had stopped off at President Eisenhower's command post on the Augusta, Georgia, golf course, so that Dulles could brief the President on the latest Soviet-Berlin ultimatum. Milton Eisenhower had flown with us as far as Augusta. Over breakfast on the plane, the President's brother had told Dulles that "Mexican culture is very much involved with their food, which is distinctive, and peculiar only to them."

Dulles hadn't been much concerned with Mexican food on the plane and had merely grunted in reply, saying, "I've got to brief the President on Berlin."

Milton Eisenhower's answer to that was, "Ike is still angry over and sensitive about the charge that he held back the Allied Armies and let the Russians sweep right through Berlin at the end of World War Two. Ike feels," he continued, "that if he'd disobeyed orders from Washington, Roosevelt would have had him in chains. Indeed, he thinks Truman would have had him shot!"

"*Shot!*" Dulles exclaimed.

"Yes!" Milton Eisenhower said, looking, somehow, smug.

"Why?" I asked.

They both looked at me as if I had just arrived from space, but Milton Eisenhower answered my question. "Ike feels that Truman doesn't like generals—*any* generals except Omar Bradley, who's from Missouri, and General

Marshall, whom he sort of promoted right up to God so he wouldn't be a general anymore."

I was surprised. Dulles was nonplussed.

Milton Eisenhower continued. "Ike feels, for instance, that Truman was right to fire MacArthur, but that he did it for the wrong reason, that he didn't really fire him for insubordination, which was the right reason, but because MacArthur was the biggest general of them all. Truman remembered him strutting around France in World War One, and, you see, the thing about MacArthur is that he *looks* so much like a general. Outstanding general. No question about that. But, Ike says, the man's ego colors everything."

Dulles muttered, "Yes, of course."

"So, you see," Milton Eisenhower concluded, "Ike will stand firm on Berlin. He won't let the Soviets bluff him."

"Yes, well," Dulles responded, "the Soviets aren't going to start a war unless they *want* a war anyway, and they won't *want* a war until they think they can win it, or, at least, until they think we think they can win it. It's just not a question of us provoking them into war. They won't be provoked. They will strike only when they judge the forces and/or the *will* opposing them to be weak."

This kind of talk seemed to make Milton Eisenhower uncomfortable. He didn't go directly back to Mexican food, but he did change the subject to Mexican agriculture, stating that the Mexicans must grow more corn, and that, in fact, if every Mexican family grew at least thirty more ears of corn, Mexico's ongoing economic crisis would become "manageable." He compared it to football, drawing a conclusion I could not comprehend. I don't think Dulles comprehended it either, but, he smiled and twitched his eyes a few times.

When we landed in Augusta, we went straight to the

golf course, where, with regard to the new Soviet threats to Berlin, Eisenhower told Dulles to "Let the Soviets make noise! That's all it is—noise. If we stand firm, that's all it will be. Noise." The President's lip curled as he repeated "Noise."

Dulles nodded agreement, and we returned to the airport and the air.

Then we were coming in over the twilight-grim vastness of Mexico's high plateau, nearly 8,000 feet above sea level. When we landed, we saw, in the mist, a lady smoking a cigar. Dulles almost shouted, "My God! Not again!"

"The Minister of Theological Affairs?" I murmured.

"Yes," he whispered, choking on the single word.

"It's not her," I said.

"Thank God," he responded.

We were both thinking of a State Dinner in Copenhagen the year before when Denmark's Minister of Theological Affairs, a granite-jawed woman of pronounced opinions, had spent a long evening burning his ear with morality and his nose with cigar smoke. The woman had really smoked a mean cigar. She stood out, even in a country where cigar-smoking women were not at all uncommon.

However, this was Mexico, and the woman in the mist with the cigar was engulfed in the crowd that threatened to swallow us up.

The scene was surreal. Dulles and Mexico's Foreign Minister were shouting at each other. The TV lights had a strange cast in the high, thin air, and the faces of the two statesmen looked purple over orange. The push and shove around us was fierce. Somebody tossed a fistful of confetti. Bands were blaring everywhere. Shouts. Color. And a clang, clang, clang. The whirl and pomp of a Spanish fiesta all blended with the plodding scream of the re-emerging Aztec soul. It was then that I first thought of having an enchilada in Mexico City, but I had to move

Dulles to the waiting limousine that my security colleague K. O. Lynch had pointed out to me. It was impossible. We were swamped in people. I noticed what appeared to be a ragtag mob in sandals, serapes, and rags bearing down on us, and I turned to the man Lynch had introduced to me as the Chief of Police, my face giving the question. The Chief, his smile pushing out from under his great moustache, screamed into my ear, *"Don't worry, don't worry*—they are all *my* men!"

It was terrifying. The Chief's "men" raged all around us, scaring everybody. I was relieved when, finally, we were racing away from the airport and into the city, but not for long. The driver took what he described as a "short cut" and we found ourselves trapped in a mob in the middle of an alley and I thought I heard a shot. I leaped from the limousine, but the Chief was right there, assuring me that it was just one of his men taking "a little target practice."

We did get out of that alley, but not before I began to question my own sanity.

It was after this, when I had seen Dulles into the well-guarded American Embassy residence, that I truly began my search for an enchilada, a search that was finally brought to a successful conclusion in the American Embassy canteen. I don't think that Dulles told the new President of Mexico about the enchilada search, which even involved his army, but he did tell him, "President Eisenhower's brother, Milton, thinks you should grow more corn."

López Mateos listened in English, and then in Spanish, and asked, "Does Dr. Eisenhower wish to *buy* our corn?"

"Oh, no," Dulles replied, "I think that he thought selling more corn might help your economy."

Mexico's new President mumbled some Spanish and looked dramatically shaken. He coughed, and consulted his interpreter, who then said to Dulles, "The President would like Dr. Eisenhower to know that there *are* Mexicans who understand the simple economic fact that if one can sell one's product, it helps one's economy."

Dulles tried to laugh, but it came out sounding like a sea lion's honk. López Mateos looked disturbed. Other than that, the shots in the alley, and the search for the perfect enchilada—which is *any* enchilada—everything went well. Except, that is, for problems with the altitude.

After we had climbed a particularly long flight of stairs, I remarked to Dulles, "I'm sure glad London isn't at this altitude."

"Why?" he asked.

I recalled to him the times the British Foreign Office elevator had broken down, forcing us to walk up the long steps, arriving at meetings with Anthony Eden, Harold Macmillan, and Selwyn Lloyd out of breath and at a disadvantage. "I've often suspected that they planned those breakdowns," I said, adding, "Diplomatic strategy."

"I've thought about that, too," he responded, without elaborating.

"You mean you've thought about the possibility that the British got you out-of-breath on purpose before talking to you?" I asked.

"Yes," he replied, with a small smile. "I have."

"We'll never know for sure," I said, "but it could be true. I asked one of my Yard friends, in a joking way, if the elevator breakdowns were planned and he said, also in a joking way, 'They want any bloody advantage they can get over bloody Dulles!'"

"Your Scotland Yard friend really said that?"

"Yes, sir."

"My, my," he mumbled. "Of course, it's always been their way to impress, intimidate, overwhelm, and . . . they can't overwhelm anymore. Can't really intimidate or impress in the old way, although, actually, they do still impress . . . pomp and, uh . . ."

"Circumstance."

"Exactly!" he said, with a chop.

All I could think of to say was, "Yes, sir."

"We've got to think this through," he went on.

"Of course," I agreed.

"We have too many elevators back in the State Department," he murmured thoughtfully.

"Sir?"

"We can't have them *all* break down at once, can we?" he asked.

"Well," I replied, "we *could* arrange to have them all break down at once, I suppose, but . . ."

He interrupted me with, "It wouldn't be nearly as effective."

"As the British?"

"Yes."

"Why not?" I asked. "Do you think that having one elevator break down is more effective than having ten elevators break down?"

"No, no," he responded. "But, there's something about that massive pile of stone of a foreign office there in London that gives such an operation the proper atmosphere, makes it seem almost . . . legitimate."

"Makes it legitimate to declare their sole elevator busted so *you* will have to walk up the steps?"

"They've done worse than that in there," he grumped.

"That's true," I agreed.

"But," he said, "I hope they don't do that to me the next time we're in London. I'm feeling the steps more these days. I'm feeling *everything* more. . . ."

He *was* feeling everything more—painfully so. He was sicker than we knew, but *he* knew and he refused to give in to it. Even so, when we left Mexico City, we did something unusual. We stopped in California so that Dulles could rest—at the Smoke Tree Ranch in Palm Springs. This was not only unusual, it was unheard of.

No business!

Just rest.

The first thing that happened to *me* at that ranch was the offer by a fine-looking young woman to take me horseback riding. I felt flattered until she told me that her ranch job was as "children's hostess." She explained that the various members of the ranch staff had been assigned to the various members of the Secretary's party, and she had "drawn" me.

"Did you actually have a drawing?" I asked her.

"No, no," she replied. "Not an actual drawing."

I was intrigued. "Then, how come *you* got *me?*"

"Well," she said, "I think we got the word that you were pretty young."

"The *child* in the group!"

She looked embarrassed, as she responded, "We didn't *know* your *actual* age."

"Somebody figured that maybe Dulles had a nine-year-old bodyguard?" I questioned.

"These days you never know," she responded with a small smirk.

What could I say to that?

I did go riding with her—western style, in my flannel slacks and loafers. She said I was very brave. I told Dulles about it and he said, "That young woman is no child."

I informed him that *she* wasn't *supposed* to be a child; that *her* job was to take care of children.

"You're certainly no child, either," he rumbled.

"She knows that!" I responded.

"That's a relief," he said, breathing deeply, as if in pain.

I grabbed his arm, worried, asking, "Are you okay?"

I think he *was* in pain, but he said, "I am in pain only when I think about that old cowboy they seem to have assigned to me the way they have assigned that children's hostess to you."

"He's the boss around here, Mr. Secretary," I said.

Dulles looked forlorn as he grumbled, "Bosses rarely look like children's hostesses do they?"

"That is certainly true," I agreed.

"Enjoy yourself, Lou," he said. "Enjoy yourself. As for me, I think I need a drink."

We had been watching the sun go down behind the mountains. He looked sad and tired, and, in the soft desert dusk, I walked him to his cottage. Pain etched his eyes. He skipped dinner in the main ranch house that night. I didn't. I went straight to the big dining room and ordered and received two cheese enchiladas.

As I wolfed down the first two of seven enchiladas, the ranch boss and some of the "hands" asked me if I'd had "any adventures" lately. I told them about the night, two months before, when Dulles' canvas bunk on a Jet Tanker bound for Rome and the funeral of Pope Pius XII collapsed. It left him lying on the deck, showing pain and sounding laughter, with Ambassador Clare Booth Luce in her nightgown peering down at him, asking, "Foster? What *are* you doing down there on the floor?"

Jet aircraft had not quite come into general use, but Dulles had had to go to the last rites for the Pope, and then, almost immediately to Taiwan. Strategic Air Command (SAC) chief, General Curtis LeMay had suggested a Jet Tanker to Rome and then over the North Pole to the Pacific as the way to do it. Not unusual in 1986. Very unusual in 1958.

LeMay had been quoted as saying, "I've been trying to get Dulles traveling in one of my aircraft for years!" When I heard these words, I thought it was vintage LeMay, but I didn't fully grasp his meaning until I met the officer who was going to be our aircraft commander. He was chewing an unlit cigar and wearing a jumpsuit tucked into spit-polished combat boots with a holstered .45 slapping at his hip. A LeMay clone. It would be as if the general was with us.

The official U.S. delegation to the Pope's funeral, led by Dulles, included John McCone and Clare Booth Luce. When we all got into the aircraft's long, barren tunnel of a cabin, I half sang to Mrs. Luce, "You're in the Strategic Air Command now." She looked at me, the pilot, and the plane, and, in a conspiratorial whisper, said, "Only for the Pope would I do something like this."

I said, with a laugh, but meaning it, "Mrs. Luce, you could probably do General LeMay's job."

"I probably could," she smiled, "but don't let it get around."

My Smoke Tree Ranch dinner companions seemed fascinated with all this. Mrs. Luce in particular caught their interest. The ranch boss asked me, "Didn't Dulles have a little, uh, sex thing with Clare Luce?"

Startled, I studied the man. His eyes were on the move, up and down, up and down. His body was a battered tube. He looked like the caterpillar in *Alice in Wonderland*, but he seemed serious, although I found his question difficult to take seriously. I said, "Couldn't be Dulles. Must have been somebody else."

"You're right!" he barked. "It was Sinatra! That's it! She was helping Sinatra! Helping him make a comeback. Giving him a boost where a guy needs it. Know what I mean? But, she did it on Dulles' orders, didn't she?"

I felt as if we were both in *Alice in Wonderland*. Sinatra had been fighting his way back from temporary eclipse in those days, but I said, "I'm sure there's nothing to *any* of that—my God, where'd you hear such an idea? *Either* idea. Dulles *or* Sinatra, or Dulles ordering her to take on Sinatra. It's crazy. I mean, Dulles certainly likes Clare Booth Luce—I've heard him call her a 'woman of great character.' As for Sinatra, Dulles once told me he liked the way that man sings 'Somewhere Over the Rainbow.' "

"'Somewhere Over the Rainbow'?" the caterpillarlike boss screeched.

"Right!" I replied.

"Impossible," the caterpillar said, with emphasis on the "im."

"Why?"

"Sinatra is not—repeat, not—a 'Somewhere Over the Rainbow' man."

"If Dulles said he heard Sinatra sing 'Somewhere Over the Rainbow,' then he heard Sinatra sing 'Somewhere Over the Rainbow'!" I said sharply, a little irritated with the guy.

"Hey, hey," he sang soothingly, "I didn't mean nothin'. The old man—Dulles—is a tough old buzzard, isn't he?"

"Yes, he is," I agreed.

"That must'a been something in that Jet Tanker—lots a room—Dulles and Clare Booth Luce in 'lots a room' . . ."

Not at all sure what the man meant, I said, "Sure, I was traveling with a taped-up sprained ankle."

"Jesus! How'd you do that?"

"I was chain-sawing a tree the night before we left, twisted my foot, and . . ."

"Maybe you're the tough one," he interrupted, "although you don't look it."

"Is that why you put me in the keeping of the children's hostess?"

"I hadn't even met you when I did that," he said, slapping me on the knee, adding, "besides, you liked her didn't you?"

"She's very nice," I responded.

"Of course, she is," he said, looking self-satisfied. "But, that sprained ankle, twisted foot—I mean, what would you have done if somebody'd attacked Dulles?"

"I'd of kicked 'em with the good foot!" I laughed.

"Sure," he said, showing his disbelief.

"The worst thing about it from my standpoint was that my doctor had taped it just right so I didn't want to tamper with it until I got back and, finally, in Taipei, I just *had* to take a bath."

"Great!" he exclaimed. "*Geisha* girls?"

"Geisha girls are in Japan, not on Taiwan," I snapped, bugged by his ignorance.

"Yeah, sure. But, why'd you take a bath in Taiwan?"

"Why'd I take a bath on Taiwan?" I whispered to myself, and said, "I took a bath because I sweat one hell of a lot of sweat thinking about how the Soviets might have shot us down coming over the North Pole—Soviet fighters all around us—and, well, you know how it is when you sweat a lot."

"How'd you manage it?" he asked.

"The Russians?"

"No, the bath!" he said, his curiosity showing.

"It was my left ankle," I said, trying to keep it simple, "so I sat in the bathtub backwards."

"You sat in a Chinese bathtub backwards?" he asked, his disbelief showing again.

"Right. With my left ankle and foot and all the tape hanging over the side of the tub, never getting near the water."

He interrupted with, "So, John Foster Dulles' bodyguard, security man—say, just what in the hell *are* you, anyway?"

"Both of those and more."

"In a Chinese bathtub, backwards." The man looked dumbfounded.

"I think the tub was made in Ohio, but that's not the point—the point is that the tape was on just right, and I wanted to keep it on, and dry, until I got back to Washington."

"I see," he said. "But, there you were, Dulles' security man, in a Chinese bathtub which was made in Ohio, with your foot hanging out, and . . . what?"

"The thing is, I had a pretty good bath and kept the tape dry, and right after the bath the Chief of Police of Taipei threw a lunch for me where one hundred and forty-three toasts were offered—seventy-seven of them to Dulles."

The man studied me and said, "I am beginning to understand."

"Understand?" I questioned.

He slapped my knee, again, saying, "Sure. Understand. Understand why you are Dulles' security man. Your mind runs in, uh, strange directions."

"Is that a compliment?"

"I don't know. Maybe. But, what about the Russians at the North Pole? I didn't quite get that." He looked genuinely puzzled.

I tried to explain it. "When we made a fueling stop at an Air Force base near Fairbanks, Alaska, Dulles got word that the Communist Chinese had *just* resumed bombardment of the offshore islands of Quemoy and Matsu, and that Soviet MIG fighters had *simultaneously* appeared over the Bering Strait near our projected flight pattern for Taiwan. Coincidence? We didn't really know, but Dulles said, 'The Russians really like to scare you if you let them!' Then he sat down and went through a bowl of salted peanuts."

The ranch boss curled and uncurled his caterpillar's body and sneezed out some words, "MIGs are buzzing around, and Dulles *ate a bowl of salted peanuts?*"

"Exactly."

"Didn't he have a drink with them?"

"He had a drink in his hand, but he held off actually drinking it and worked his finger around in the ice cubes and licked his finger and ate some nuts."

"Licked the booze off his finger?"

"Right," I responded, holding back a laugh.

He was definitely not laughing as he asked, "You're telling me that while the Chinese are shooting off cannons and the Russians are sending up fighters in front of him, Dulles is licking booze off his finger?"

"You've got it."

He couldn't decide whether he should take me seriously or not, but he pursued it. "Where were you? In some kind of secret command post, or underground center, or something like that?"

"Nothing like that. More like a motel bedroom—one of those Air Force officer's 'suites.'"

His eyes bored into me. "So, what happened?"

"Dulles said that 'of course' we were going on—'Let's just *see* if those MIGs'll shoot at us' he said—but he thought he'd better check in with President Eisenhower, and, maybe, make a statement. So it was two in the morning, Alaska time, and five in the morning in Denver, where President Eisenhower was, and the Air Force put the call through, getting a Secret Service agent on the other end, and Dulles grabbed the phone, shouting, 'Hello! Hello . . . yes, this is Secretary Dulles . . . Dulles! . . . *Dulles!* Yes, speaking . . . no, no, no, *Secretary of State* Dulles! That's right, I am the Secretary of State . . . yes, I know it's still dark there. It's dark, here, too. That's right, the President. Yes, I want to speak with him, and . . . yes, yes, you'd better wake him up . . . please . . . yes, I said wake him up . . . thank you . . . Hello, Mr. President! . . . Yes! This is Foster.'"

"You mean he woke Eisenhower *up?*" the ranch boss asked, his eyes glistening.

"Yes," I said. "I'm trying to give you the feel of Dulles' side of the conversation."

"You couldn't hear Eisenhower?"

"No, just Dulles' end of it. And, he said, 'Mr. President, this is Foster.' Then, he shouted, *'Foster!'* and told him, 'I'm in Alaska . . . *Alaska!'* and went on with 'Yes, Mr. President, it's pretty cold, here, but how are you? Good! You know I'm flying on to Taiwan to see Chiang. . . . No, Chiang is not in Alaska, but I've just learned that the Communist Chinese have just started firing at the off-shore islands again, apparently in my honor. Yes,' he said after Eisenhower said something, 'and there are apparently a few MIGs flying around in the air up here, and . . . what? . . . yes,' Dulles laughed 'I'm getting a Soviet escort, but I do feel I should go on, no question about it. Yes, definitely, I must, I've got a statement here, and, yes . . . I'd like to read it to you.'"

As I recalled Dulles' end of that conversation, the ranch table around me was silent, until the ranch boss jumped in with, "Eisenhower thought Chiang Kai-shek was in Alaska?"

"He might have, but I think he was joking," I replied. "Remember, Dulles woke him up."

"And you guys went on—right through the Russian MIGs?"

"Yes, we went on . . . right through the Russian MIGs."

"And you got your bath?"

"And I got my bath."

He laughed, really laughed. "Bet they don't have any enchiladas on Taiwan?"

"Probably not. But I did get some on a submarine base without submarines in Pakistan."

"Enchiladas in Pakistan?"

"Yes."

He touched my knee. It wasn't a slap this time. It was a touch, and he said, admiration showing, "You really are devious, aren't you?"

"That's what Dulles said," I smiled.

"That's what the woman who was asking about you said."

"What woman?"

"The one who looks just like Marilyn Monroe."

My stomach clenched and unclenched like a fist.

11

Diplomacy by Other Means— A Not-So-Humorous Speculation

The Lady of the Lake hid for a time, somewhere down deep in the cellar of my mind. I forgot about her. But, I was to see her one more time, and it was frightening. To put it into context, I must tell a story that I know is bizarre, and, unlike other portions of this book, hardly humorous. It is a story that I have kept in the closet for many years. It starts, I suppose, on a lovely spring day just outside Paris.

Dulles and I were walking on the clipped green lawn of the Trianon Palace at Versailles. The breeze around us was frisky, the air French magic. Even today, I can feel it. Dulles' friend of many years, Jean Monnet (a.k.a. "Mr. Europe" and "Brandy Man"), had just bowed, waved, and, in English, whispered, "Farewell, dear friend." Other words flowed softly out with an accent that can only be described as verbal perfume as the old French statesman eased his legs away. Old bones and old manners, I thought. Their parting could have occurred in a room lit by gas lamps.

As Monnet trudged away, Dulles talked about Versailles's Hall of Mirrors, where we had just had lunch. He said that after World War I, "We signed the Treaty of Versailles, thinking we were going to end war, right there, in the Hall of Mirrors, where we lunched today." His eyes filmed over, as he continued, "So many things went wrong after that. Force continued to be the most effective method of change, and we cannot lay the blame for that *entirely* at the doorsteps of Hitler, Stalin, or Hirohito."

Listening to Dulles talk about great events and the people who influence them, my mind flashed on poet Ezra Pound. As a student studying literature at Washington, D.C.'s George Washington University in 1950, I had visited Pound at the District of Columbia (Federal) Insane Asylum, St. Elizabeth's, where he was then incarcerated. A famous, if controversial, literary figure for decades, Pound had broadcast on Radio Rome during World War II and been declared insane after the U.S. Army returned him from Italy. When I joined the diverse group that visited him at St. Elizabeth's, he talked poetry and told about friends he had helped, like T. S. Eliot and Ernest Hemingway. He also preached what was then regarded as right-wing politics, although poet Allen Ginsberg has said that Pound was actually "of the Left" and "ahead of his time." In any case, Pound loved to say that Woodrow Wilson's confidant, Colonel E. M. House, set up the "secret" Council on Foreign Relations after World War I to "steer" America into a "world socialist" conspiracy that was "not socialist at all." To buttress such convoluted thinking, he would say that it all had to do with Cecil Rhodes and his "diamond mines and scholarships," and "the Rothschilds, and the British and American 'establishments,'" which, he said, had "joined forces" to carry out the aims of a "hidden force" that went "deep into history."

Walking the grounds of the Trianon Palace, I told Dulles about Pound and asked him about Colonel House and the "secret doings" of the Council on Foreign Relations.

He responded with a question. "Pound's an anti-Semite, isn't he?"

"I think he is," I replied, "but he would tell you he was talking about forces, not people."

Dulles' walk was sometimes a lurch. He lurched, snorting, "Forces! Harumph! What's *that* mean?"

"I'm not sure," I said, "but, when I told Pound that I went to a Washington, D.C., high school that was almost seventy percent Jewish, and that I was at least seventeen before I realized that 'they' weren't the majority and that 'we' weren't the minority, he got very excited and said, 'That accounts for it! I thought you *seemed* a little Jewish.' When I asked the old poet how I could 'seem' a 'little' Jewish, he told me not to worry about it, that with a name like Jefferson, coupled with seeming a little Jewish, I had a 'winning combination.' If I 'put my mind to it,' he said, I 'couldn't be stopped.'"

"Stopped from doing what?" Dulles asked.

"He never told me," I replied.

"Amazing," Dulles murmured, sounding truly amazed.

"Pound *is* amazing," I agreed. "He wrote some really fine poetry, and influenced some of the best writers of his generation. But, well, he does mix in quite a bit of junk."

Dulles liked the word "junk." He rolled it around on his tongue. "Junk, huh? Junk. Yes. Indeed, yes. Junk. Indeed, yes. Junk." Then, he asked, "Is the man *really* crazy?"

"Maybe, a little, now . . ." I replied, trying to answer the question for myself as well as for Dulles.

"Was he crazy when they put him in there?"

"I don't know," I said. "I don't think so."

Dulles raised one eyebrow, lowered it, and raised the other. The wrinkles on his forehead winked, as he said, "Strange that you knew him."

"Yes, sir. But what *about* Colonel House and the 'secret doings' of the Council on Foreign Relations?"

Dulles gave another lurch and guffawed, "Nothing secret about it. I was right there *with* House at the beginning. Many of us were—all filled with idealism."

"What about John Maynard Keynes?" I asked. "Pound said that Keynes was 'sinister,' that Keynes' whole idea was that countries could borrow their way into prosperity and that Keynes 'got *that* ball rolling' during the writing of the Treaty of Versailles."

Dulles sniffed, and said, "Keynes was hardly 'sinister.'"

"But, he did believe that nations could borrow their way into prosperity, didn't he?"

Dulles sniffed again. "Something like that."

"Didn't Keynes say something about capitalism being 'extraordinary' because it assumed that 'the nastiest of men for the nastiest of motives' would somehow work for the benefit of all?"

Dulles gargled out a big laugh. "Keynes may have said that; he may well have. Sounds like him. I knew him, you know. For years. We didn't agree too much, but I liked him. Civilized fella, but, well, he was sorta like a thumbnail without the thumb. Waved his fingers around a lot."

"Not his thumbs?"

"No," he said, laughing, "not his thumbs."

"But a lot of the things Pound sees as 'sinister' started right here in the Hall of Mirrors, I guess."

"Yes," he agreed, "a lot of it started right here. Good Lord! The Right and the Left and who knows who—to them it's 'secret' and 'sinister' and . . . my God, there's nothing to it. Sure, the *whole world* wasn't involved.

Maybe they should have been—lot of the decisions made here didn't turn out too well. We put Germany down so far—shackled 'em up—that they were ready and ripe for Hitler. But, people with the 'large view' or whatever you want to call it have *always* made the decisions, always run things—men of affairs—I mean, what do you think the Soviet leaders are? They're Communists, yes, but, *all* Communists do not run the Soviet Union, and, if you are *not* a Communist, from the standpoint of the decision-making process, you do not exist."

I nodded and remarked, "People of shared interests tend to act together."

Dulles' whole face scrunched upward. I could see his thoughts wrinkling right through the skin on his forehead. Indeed, his forehead appeared to be under great stress as it strained to disappear beyond his hairline. I had never seen him look more serious as he said, "The Soviets take the long view—most Americans find that nearly impossible—and, believe me, the Soviets do not let Communist ideology interfere with that long view." I must have looked puzzled, because he quickly added, "I know it sounds strange. If you read Lenin and Stalin, you can understand it."

I boiled it down to, "They take the view that if you have to shoot *one* Communist to make *two* Communists, then, of course, you shoot one Communist."

"Very good," he said, approvingly. "Excellent way to put it. I remember, in 1947, a crucial year for Europe, but, anyway, Mrs. Dulles and I were staying at Claridge's in London at a time when Paris was coming apart. Everything in Paris, from power plants to the government, had apparently broken down, but details were scanty, and George Marshall—he was Secretary of State at that point—asked me to go over and have a look and report back to him. He was afraid the Communists were about to take over. The pretext for our trip was that we were going over to buy Janet a hat. She got upset about that—too frivolous, she said—and she insisted on leaving some papers at Claridge's that would show, in case something happened to us, that we hadn't gone over just to buy her a hat."

"Nobody would have taken such an idea—that you went over just to buy Mrs. Dulles a hat—seriously, would they?" I asked.

"Buying a hat can be a very serious business!" he said, with a straight face, going on, "Anyway, we took the boat train, but before the train got to Paris, the tracks ahead of us were blown up and we were rerouted. It took quite some time, but we finally got into Paris and the lights were out and the water had stopped. Soldiers were at the railroad stations and revolutionaries were marching the streets singing "The Internationale." It was terrible. Terrible. I met with what I could find of the government, the opposition. Then, in an apartment that was sort of hidden away, I met with General de Gaulle, and he told me that they would get through it, that France was 'safe' for the moment because, for one thing, the Soviets *did* desire a 'move to the Left' in France that would be a thorn in our sides, but that they were not ready to have France become a 'Communist State' yet, and so, he said, for the moment they would sacrifice a few Communists—quite a few Communists—for what they deemed their long-term interest."

Surprised, I said, "And all this time I thought that what happened in France in those days was a defeat for the Communists."

"That's the trouble," he crunched. "Most people see just what they see and that's it. They don't see behind things, under them, around them. It's like those people who say my target all my life was to be Secretary of State! Ridiculous. I *am* Secretary of State, but you'd be crazy, just plain crazy, to set your sights on only one thing to the exclusion of everything else. There are just too many things involved."

"The endless journey to Oz . . ." I mumbled.

"What did you say?" he questioned, sharply.

"I'm not sure," I responded, meaning it.

"Yes, well, if I've had an objective, it's been to be of service, to make the world a little better, peaceful, do what I could, find mechanisms, instruments, institutions, organizations, groups to further the effort . . . the effort for peace. And, it does take effort, to keep the peace. But, when people are in groups, talking, they generally aren't fighting. Seems simple, doesn't it, but, people, in their perpetual search for unattainable and ultimate solutions, don't really think about these things, simple things, like just keeping the conversation going. And America has a short memory, or, at least, many Americans have short memories." He chuckled. "Maybe that's why some of these things—the Council on Foreign Relations, the United Nations—seem so secret, so sinister to some of these extremists. Short memories."

"You don't exactly sound 'sinister,'" I said, lightly.

"I certainly hope not!" he almost shouted. "My heavens, I recognize the inequities that occur in the world—*everywhere* in the world. Life is harder for some, easier for some. Opportunities differ. Of course they do. Always have. But there *are* opportunities in the United States. *That* is the point. There *are* opportunities. And we have freedom—choice, the right to choose. That is what freedom is all about. Choice. But! . . . you haven't been to Moscow, have you?"

"No, I haven't."

"It's terrible. Not just in the material sense. It's the whole Soviet theory of fear as a motivating force. They isolate people from people, country from country—tie it all together—terrible."

Again lightly, "Mr. Secretary, you do not sound much like a leader of the 'world socialist conspiracy.' Hard to believe there are people in this country who actually see you that way."

He frowned. "I know. It's amazing." He paused and pointed, saying, "See that little road down there? Well, Mrs. Dulles and I used to come here with the children— before we could really afford it—and they'd bring the children right up that road in donkey carts." He was quiet for a moment, lost in thoughts of the past. Then, his mind snapped sharply into the present. He growled, "Ridiculous! Some people, these right-wingers, think I'm actually soft on Communism." He coughed up a sour laugh, pinched his nose, and went on, "Can you *imagine* that? Good Lord! And, on the other side, the Left, I'm the 'Mad Bomber,' even though I keep a tight, tight hold on the bombs. Those left-wing fellas think I'm the Secretary of State from Wall Street, or 'the moneychangers,' as your friend Pound might put it. Where do they think most of my predecessors for the past hundred years or so have came from? It's a good training ground. You learn how to deal with the real world. Not the world you'd like to see, necessarily. The world that *is*. And as to House and the Council on Foreign Relations and the rest, well, Pound forgot about his fellow writer, H. G. Wells. Wells was very influential. Strong on Anglo-American relations as a way to further his views of progress. He wanted one common and final supreme court for the whole world, probably with himself in charge. But the Anglo-American thing, well, I've always been more comfortable, felt more at home, here in France. Not all that common among Americans." A laugh erupted, as he concluded, "Particularly us Wall Streeters."

We had reached a corner of the lawn that had apparently decided to die. The green was gone. It wasn't even brown. It was gray. Our walk had stretched beyond the sprinkler line, and a lady with purple eyebrows, a long muslin dress, and a wolfhound came out from behind a hedge and gasped. The dog looked ready to attack. It growled. Its teeth began to chatter, sounding like a drawerful of kitchen knives. I grabbed Dulles' arm and moved him back behind the safety of the sprinkler line. "*Who* was that woman?" he asked.

"I like French women!" I answered, not exactly directing myself to his question.

"That's a different subject."

"It's related."

"Oh?"

"Mr. Secretary, did you ever feel, uh, 'at home' with a French woman—say, back in those days when you used to put on that hat and go out and riot in Paris?"

Dulles' face really twitched on that one. "Well, certainly, yes, that is . . ." His voice wandered away, but returned strongly with, "As a matter of fact, there was an Englishwoman, too, but that, of course, was all long before I met Mrs. Dulles."

"I see." I chuckled. "But, you've always felt more comfortable in France. Interesting. Sort of a throwback to the Founding Fathers. They felt more comfortable in France— liked it better. But, you were talking about H. G. Wells, the Council . . ."

"Yes," he responded. "People who say that the Council on Foreign Relations and such are instruments to run the world's affairs are, in one sense . . . well, they're right, although, perhaps, for the wrong reasons." He snorted, and shuffled his big, bony body around in one of those expensively tailored, but strangely fitting green suits he favored (a fitter at New York's Brooks Brothers once told

201

me that "Foster Dulles likes the *idea* of good clothing more than he likes good clothing") and continued. "Certainly it all has something to do with business and finance. One way or another, that's what makes much of the world go 'round—business and finance. And I for one find the desire for gain a more desirable motivating factor than fear. Does that make me Right, or Left, or what?"

"Well," I said, "you are not exactly popular with the Left *or* the Right at the moment."

His eyes were scanning the clear sky. The lady with the wolfhound paraded sedately by, the dog's mouth still and wet. Dulles' eyes followed them. His face flicked around in emotions infrequently exhibited. Finally, he said softly, "Makes it tough on *you*, I guess—all these people who seem to hate me. I suppose a lot of people would feel better if I just weren't around anymore. Certainly some of the Soviets would—they just as much as say it. And, who's that nut who says I'm trying to make the world 'safe for greed'? Well, he's right. I am. Safe for greed and giving and peace and living . . . but, yes, the Soviets . . ."

"The Soviets are certainly capable of it."

"Killing me?"

"Yes."

"I know. And, yet, there are those people who say I'm running the State Department with Communists! Can you imagine it? *Me! Running the State Department with Communists! Wall Street, Communists, and me." His laugh stopped in his stomach. He rubbed his nose and concluded, "Actually, it's hard to say *who* might want to take a shot at me."

Nobody took a shot at him.

He died of cancer.

His first operation occurred in 1956.

The cancer flared up again in 1958, and he was dead in 1959.

And, when they buried him at Arlington National Cemetery, I saw, or thought I saw, in the large crowd at graveside, smiling, the Lady of the Lake. Her smile, if it was her, made me angry. With all his warts, I had come to respect Dulles. Hell, I loved the guy. Under that tough exterior I had found a man of peace, and, more importantly, a man who understood what it took to *keep* peace. I had also found a man who felt deeply and, at his family's request, I had spent his last months taking rides with him in the park, watching him die. I was touched deeply, so deeply that I tried to put my thoughts to paper and came up with a piece that, although it seems somewhat sophomoric today, nevertheless, for me, recalls how affected I was. It started:

> Rides in the park with the dying American, his
> shirt collars growing ever looser. Brief moments of
> peace. His remark to his wife that the way the
> press was complimenting him, he *"must"* be dying.
> The drawn and humbled face of the President of
> the United States leaving the hospital room with
> the gift of a book on Communism under his arm.
> The hymns of enduring faith echoing in the
> corridors. Plaintive sounds which still resound in
> memory's very personal ear. And then the chair
> was vacant. . . . our nation's high councils had lost
> the vital force . . .

So, I was furious at the graveside smile of the lady who looked like the Lady of the Lake, but, as before, she disappeared, and I was left with my fury, my sadness, and a question—was she merely a figment of a fevered imagination that belonged to me, or could she have been involved in Dulles' death? Or both? Or what?

About six months before Dulles' death, we had noticed

that the Soviet security people were using Geiger counters
to check the food served to their leaders. Indeed, at a
Washington dinner in January 1959 for long-time Soviet
trade chief, Anastas Mikoyan—one of the last official dinners Dulles attended—Soviet security asked us to furnish
Geiger counters and then brought their own and used
both to check all food going in Mikoyan's direction. Actually, they didn't operate our Geiger counter. They just followed it. One of my State Department security colleagues,
John Abidian, swooped it in over Mikoyan's food while
murmuring to himself, "If my mother could only see me
now. If my mother could only see me now." John, like
Mikoyan, was of Armenian heritage, and his mother was
convinced that whenever he was around Mikoyan, he was
there for one reason—to play pinochle with the Soviet
leader. Pinochle was like a national game with Armenians
and, from Abidian's mother's standpoint, why else would
her son be around Mikoyan? Later, when Abidian was assigned to Moscow as the American Embassy security officer, his mother believed, or so he told me, that the
United States Government was sending him there for the
sole purpose of playing pinochle with Mikoyan. Why else?
In fact, his mission was to make one room in the Embassy
a safe place to talk without Soviet ears in the walls. Besides, he was working for an Ambassador—Llewellyn
Thompson—who loved poker. John, a linguist, diplomat,
and fine security officer, became, in short order, an outstanding poker player and member of Ambassador
Thompson's exclusive weekly poker game. I don't think he
ever did play pinochle with Mikoyan, though. In any case,
as he waved his Geiger counter over Mikoyan's food that
night in Washington, I assured him that I would use all
the powers at my command to convince Dulles that
Mikoyan should be engaged in a game of pinochle. And,
although it was after Dulles had resigned as Secretary of

State, and shortly before his death, I did tell him about Mikoyan, John Abidian, and pinochle. He was intrigued and said that perhaps that was the explanation for the fact that Mikoyan had been the Soviets most effective trade negotiator for many years. Mikoyan, he said, knew "how to act quickly when it was necessary to act" and "finish matters when the time comes to finish matters," unlike "some Soviet negotiators, who just let things go on and on, afraid to make a decisive move . . . Perhaps," he concluded, "we're dealing here with a difference between pinochle-thinking and chess-thinking."

That conversation occurred during a ride in Washington's Rock Creek Park. We had parked the car, and the driver was walking Dulles' French poodle, Pepin, while we talked. It was a strange, poignant, and moving conversation. He rambled on about the Soviets and the need to "understand that they do not think as we do," but that "you *can* deal with them, and we *must* deal with them, somehow, if we are to have peace and not the end of the world."

I was not accustomed to hearing him talk about the end of the world. "Sir," I said, "I know that your illness . . ."

"*Illness!*" he thundered, the effort almost too much for him, "I'm not ill! I'm dying."

"Yes, sir," I said, worried about him, "I just thought, that is, the 'end of the world' . . . and . . . such . . ."

His voice was a growl. "I just regret that I won't be here to try and stop it."

"You've accomplished a great deal."

"I've kept the peace . . . during my watch," he said quietly, satisfaction touching the sadness in his eyes. "But," he continued, something of the old force still there, "you don't just *make* peace, now and forever, and sit back and eat . . . lotus nuts . . ."

"Lotus nuts?"

"Lotus something," he grumped. "You know," he added, "I'm deeply grateful to *you* . . . for . . . everything."

I choked up. "It's been a privilege."

"Thank you. Yes. Keeping the peace is a process, a process that goes on, and on. The . . . watch must be kept."

"It will, Mr. Secretary, it will!" I said, trying to sound cheerful.

"I pray it is so, Lou. I really am grateful to you, you know. You've lightened some of my days, and . . . you've . . . kept me alive against everything, but something beyond the control of both of us . . ."

Something beyond the control of both of us.

Geiger counters.

I did not really focus on the implications of those Geiger counters until after Dulles' death. It was difficult for me at first. History is a long cloak with many patches. They cover all manner of things. Earthshaking happenings and trivia. I had avoided looking under the Lady of the Lake patch. I did, finally, look under the Geiger-counter patch about six months after the burial at Arlington, when I discussed with a shadowy character I shall call Elmer the many times Dulles had eaten Soviet food. At first, I just wanted to talk—to bleed out the reality of Dulles' death. Words spilled down from my mind into my mouth, and Elmer listened. An unusual man. He had served in a number of security agencies and had been in Warm Springs when Franklin Roosevelt died. He seemed to have a way of being "there" when things happened. More importantly, his brain cells were file cabinets, filled with secrets. I had shared a few of those secrets over the years and thought I knew him, but he jolted me with the flat-out statement that, "Of course the Soviets murdered Dulles. He was in their way." I stared. Elmer went on, "Dulles was in the way of quite a few people. He had principles. He was trying to practice them. And he tried to see what was there, not what he wanted to be there. Dangerous stuff. Besides, he didn't mind being unpopular if it helped maintain peace."

"He didn't *like* being unpopular!" I interjected.

"Of course he didn't, but he knew it was part of the price. All these prima donnas running around don't understand that, do they? But, the murder—undoubtedly the Soviets."

"And the Soviets don't want peace?"

Elmer barked, "Everything is war with the Soviets until everything is settled on their terms."

We talked on about the many ways to kill. The KGB, for example, has reportedly subjected thallium to intense atomic radiation and put the resulting particles into the food of its victims. I can still hear Elmer saying, "It's just not all that difficult to induce cancer."

I told him about the Lady of the Lake and asked him if he thought I was imagining the whole thing. He responded with, "If you're imagining something like that, then it's something that they *want* you to imagine."

"'They' being the Soviets?" I asked.

"Probably."

"Maybe *'they'* want me to imagine that I'm going crazy."

"Maybe."

"Maybe I *am* going crazy."

Elmer stood up, and paced, saying, "You've been under a terrific strain. Moscow is making studies of how to urge that sort of thing along."

"'Strain'?"

"Sure. It's much more effective to enlarge on something that's already there than to have to start from scratch, and, if you're stretched thin, anyway, and you start seeing Ladies of the Lake . . ."

I jumped in with, "Whatever else there is to it, that woman *was* in my room in Geneva!"

"I believe it," he said, adding, "And, then there are drugs . . ."

Incredulous, I said, "You think they used drugs on *me?*"

"Probably not," he said, thoughtfully, "but, this cancer thing with Dulles, well, you can enlarge on cancer that's already there just as easily as with 'strain' or a nervous condition and you can induce cancer, or . . . there are lots of combinations."

"You really think Dulles' death was murder?"

"Don't you?"

I didn't know what I thought. I asked, "What about Eisenhower's heart attack?"

Elmer was still pacing as he responded, "I don't think they want to get rid of Eisenhower—the Soviets, that is."

"He doesn't think the Soviets want to get rid of him, either."

My pacing friend barked the question, "Eisenhower *said* that?"

"Yes. I heard him say they'd rather have somebody like him in charge here, somebody they know can't be pushed too far, rather than somebody who'd back down halfway, and then knee-jerk us all into war."

"That's really interesting. Who'd he say that to?"

"Dulles. I also heard him say one time that 'Foster Dulles keeps the Soviets on their toes for me.'"

Elmer laughed. "Maybe the Soviets decided that Foster Dulles had them too far *back* on their toes."

"God," I said, "you really *do* think they murdered him."

"Like I told you, it's easy to induce cancer."

In less than two years, Elmer was dead of cancer. His daughter later told me that he died convinced "that he was put out of the way." This came back to me when I began to read speculation that cancer had been induced in Jack Ruby to "get him out of the way" so that he could not tell the full story of Lee Harvey Oswald and the assassination of John F. Kennedy.

Strange time.

Just before Elmer died, there was the chalk-faced man of about thirty who sat next to me at a beer bar in Virginia and, in a last-gasp voice, jerked out the words, "With Dulles you must look more deeply—over your shoulder. Get to Elmer before it's too late!" As a response formed in my mouth, he tipped his glass of beer into my lap and, when my eyes went down to the sudden soak, he dashed out of the bar and disappeared.

I did not see that man again for sixteen years when, for a brief moment, I thought I saw him in Paris. We were staying in the Paris Sheraton off Tour Montparnasse—a mixed bag of a neighborhood of narrow dingy streets, boarded-up shop fronts, condemned buildings, headshops, fly-by-night galleries, and cheap bars and restaurants. It was on one of those narrow streets, actually a cobbled alley, that I saw him. He started in at the other end, gave me a look of pure hatred, shouted something that sounded like Elmer and ran. I did not see him again, although my eyes never stopped looking.

But back to 1960. After a number of conversations with Elmer, I developed a scenario, in fiction form, of what might have happened. It was circulated to a select few and became known as the "M" paper ("Made in Moscow"). But assassination was not accepted in the United States in 1961 to the extent that it is today, so, what follows was locked up for more than twenty years. As you read it, merely substitute *John Foster Dulles* for *George Wilson Fitch*.

The "M" Paper (1961)

I

George Wilson Fitch, Secretary of State, stood just inside the open door of the exclusive club on Washington's "F" Street, a few blocks from the Department of State. His smile was cold, perhaps from the snow flakes blowing in from the narrow street, as he looked down on the Member of the Presidium of the Soviet Union, his ranking guest, coming up the steps. After the briefest of greetings, they joined the other guests.

For a gathering of Soviet and American officials, the atmosphere was remarkably relaxed. It was a period of the carrot in Soviet policy, soon, to be sure, to be replaced by the stick. But, for the moment, the carrot was dominant.

The grinning Soviet Ambassador slapped the back of a prominent senator. This particular senator was impressed, as in his mind, he wrote his weekly newsletter to his constituents, stating that he has learned, through exhaustive personal contact, that, with just a little more understanding on our part, we might bring the Soviets around to *our* way of thinking.

While the guests, in small, businesslike groups, loosened up with the aid of the Washington cocktail habit, an American security officer, followed closely by a Soviet security officer, waved the wand of a Geiger counter over food to be eaten by the high Soviet official. This was being done at the urgent request of the Soviet security contingent.

The American security officers were both baffled

and amused over this latest idiosyncrasy of their
Soviet counterparts. But, with their normal good
nature, they went along with it, one sarcastically
observing, "What do they think now? That we're
going to put something *radioactive* in their boss's
food?"

There was a burst of incredulous laughter.

And standing off in a corner with a close
adviser, the man who has come to be known as the
"Conscience of the West," George Wilson Fitch, the
heavily built and sober-faced American Secretary
of State, was heard to remark, "We must be
careful now, more careful than ever. The Soviets
feel that they're on the track of something.
Something has given them reason to believe that
this is a good time to begin a tactical shift. I
wonder what that something can be."

II

A short time before Secretary Fitch's dinner for
the Presidium member, two officers of the Soviet
Secret Police met, as was their morning custom,
in a drab room in one of Moscow's already
decaying Soviet-modern buildings. This particular
building, on a narrow *sretenka* near Red Square,
was much like its immediate neighbors, except for
the two impassive, burp gun–armed sentries at its
gates.

The grim simplicity of the room inside—room
202—stood in stark contrast to the brilliant
uniforms of its occupants. There was dejection,
though, on their egg-shaped faces, a dejection that
was quite in keeping with their surroundings.

One of them—Comrade Major Fyodor

Pavlovitch Golensky—sat just next to a cluster of
battered file cabinets, chair tilted back to the wall
under a large, square space where grime has not
yet clouded the neuter-green paint. He thought
deeply about that forlorn space, where, for so
many years, the face of Stalin had gazed down
with approval on the activities of his organization,
one of the most secret and feared groups in the
Soviet bureaucracy—Moscow's Murder
Incorporated. He knew that they were still feared,
still important, but business was slow.

"Ah, Stalin," he murmured nostalgically.
Khrushchev was prominently displayed on
another wall, and, of course, there was Lenin.
Bulganin had been there for a time. No longer. He
had never amounted to much anyway. But Stalin!
Hah! Everybody was now publicly disowning
Stalin. The way things seemed to be going they all
might end up under the squinting eyes of the
dread Trotsky. If only there was a real business at
hand, he thought. An operation. Something in
which he could lose himself. Not just Jewish
doctors or a knife in some alley. No, a real
business! Maybe a big American.

The phone on the large, plain, functional desk
across from him quivered. His superior, Comrade
Colonel Yakov Petrovitch Yatselev put aside the
Albanian report on which he had been trying,
unsuccessfully, to concentrate—those crazy
mountaineers—and lazily picked up the receiver.

As it arrived at his ear, his lassitude vanished—
instantly! His whole body, without changing
position, came to attention. Hastily putting his
free hand over the mouthpiece, he whispered to
Golensky, "It is the Comrade General calling."

Then, his shaven head bobbing back like a soccer
ball just put into play, he boomed into the phone,
"Da, Comrade General!"

Although the Comrade General held Yatselev's
ear for only two minutes, it seemed, to Golensky,
much longer. An eternity! Finally, Yatselev,
handling the phone like some sacred ikon from
former times, returned it slowly to its old-
fashioned cradle and sat back in his chair,
clasping stubby fingers over an ample stomach.
An indefinable energy suddenly emanated from
his great motionless layers of fat. The puffy face of
this Commissar too long from the field came alive.
The sea-blue eyes of the killer whose function is to
plan, rather than carry out, murder sparkled. He
fingered the picturesque Order of Lenin, which
hung from his spotless tunic and then, with slow
precision, he lit one of those long, cardboard tubes
with a dash of tobacco at the end.

Golensky waited.

Somewhere a clock ticked. One of those ersatz
Swiss jobs from East Germany.

The pleasant voice of a girl sounded from the
corridor, as she urgently called to a companion
that they must hurry or the best of the food in the
special KGB cafeteria would be gone.

Golensky knew this girl, knew her deep down in
his melancholy soul. He was glad to hear her
being so practical, going to the cafeteria. Their bill
that evening would not be so large.

The sound of her footsteps disappeared.

The clock ticked on. Golensky's thoughts
caressed the fine nylons he was going to present to
the girl in the hall—but, maybe not. Perhaps he
would not present them to her. He looked over at

213

Yatselev. The Comrade Colonel was blowing smoke rings, lost in thought.

A picture of nylon stockings tightly looped around Yatselev's neck idled its way through Golensky's wandering mind. But, then, there were, of course, better uses for fine nylons—getting them on shapely female legs so that you could turn right around and get them off. Strange when you thought about it. Working so hard to get them on a woman's legs all the while wondering if you would be able to take them off. Like roulette in a way. Yes, like roulette. The girl, for instance. But, not just the girl. His whole life. Like roulette. Like the nylon stockings, it could go either way. Unless, of course, you fixed the wheel or the girl.

Who was it who was always talking about roulette? Dostoevsky? Yes. Golensky remembered. It was Dostoevsky. But was Dostoevsky respectable, now? That he couldn't remember. Not important. Roulette. *That* was the thing. That was life. The only difference was that when he *risked* his life, he always got someone else. Always. That was a difference. And, there was that professional satisfaction of a job well done; not just the bourgeois gambler's simple sense of risk. That truly was a difference. This thought gave him a feeling of enormous self-satisfaction.

His ears came alive.

Yatselev said, "The Comrade General has just returned from a meeting of the Presidium itself."

"The Presidium, itself?" Golensky shuddered.

Yatselev's reply was filled with great pomposity. "Yes, the Presidium, itself. They have ordered an operation."

"The Presidium has ordered an operation?"

"Not precisely." Yatselev measured his words. "But, yes, it will be, shall we say, an operation of sorts—against the Americans!"

Golensky muffled his shriek. "For us?" His blood ran fast. "Against the Americans?"

Yatselev crushed his cigarette in a heavy ashtray, stood, and walked to the window without speaking. The street below was ugly, brightened only by a crust of ice and snow. The vast open space of Red Square lay beyond. In the distance, he could make out the Kremlin spires, their colors blinding in the white light. Finally, ready to talk, and gaining an extra sense of authority with a glance at the silent phone—his line to those spires—he turned to Golensky, "Comrade, as you know, our policies toward the Americans have been complicated of late by this Secretary of . . ."

There was a knock at the door.

A baggy trousered, bespectacled civilian entered. With a nudge to his forehead—a cross between a salute and the British worker's ancient habit of a reach to the forelock—he announced, his accent echoing the far reaches of the Russian steppe, "Comrade Colonel," extending a black folder, *"from the Comrade General!"*

Yatselev and Golensky both exhibited their most alert, commissarlike expressions. They knew that this obsequious, crude messenger was in fact "the one" who watched over them, *and* the Comrade General, for the only office in the Kremlin that they had never entered. It was an obscure office, not listed in any registers or records, that gave Yatselev and Golensky a constriction of the mind and heart, a gnawing fear that was always with them.

Both Yatselev and Golensky frequently speculated on who might watch over this dark group that watched over them. Someone must. Everybody was watched. That was the system. But, who? Invariably they came to the conclusion that it was probably for the best that they did not know.

The peasant from the steppe gave them a steel-toothed grin reminiscent of the buffoons you could still see in Turkestan and added, "Comrade Colonel, the Comrade General wishes you to act with dispatch in this matter."

Yatselev, with an impatient shrug to his shoulders, but a polite cast of face, replied, "Yes, yes, of course. Tell the Comrade General that I *understand.*"

The baggy-trousered messenger left, smiling with the anticipation of one who has seen the first act of an amusing drama and has helped to raise the curtain on the second.

Yatselev opened a bottle of vodka and filled two glasses, handing one to Golensky.

With a single, simultaneous motion, both glasses were emptied.

Nursing his refill, Yatselev began: "What, comrade, is the most worrisome factor to us in the formulation of our American policy?"

Golensky, savoring the vodka, "Their . . . air force?"

Yatselev's hand came down hard on the desk. "No! No, comrade, no."

"Well, that is," Golensky fumbled, "perhaps, uh, their intelligence services."

"No! Comrade, dear comrade, no, no, no. Their intelligence operators, with a few exceptions, are naive. *You understand?* Naive. They are children, playing with money. Playing. Full of decadent principles, which, of course, is well for us. But, no, it is their Secretary of State, George Wilson Fitch."

"Fitch?" Golensky became thoughtful. "I see. Yes. He *is* worrisome, I suppose. Always calling the Motherland names, lies. Hurling threats. But, he's not even popular in his own country, is he?"

Yatselev leaned across the desk, his voice an ominous whisper, "Now, listen very closely. The Presidium, this morning, advised the Comrade General of their great concern over Fitch. You understand? The Presidium's great concern. Of course there are those in Fitch's own country who are also concerned. Not just those who are with us. Fitch is in their way, too. But, we, here—you, comrade, and I—are only concerned with the Presidium. They believe that Fitch has some understanding of our policy, that he alone can carry the whole imperial alliance with him. In short, he is in *our* way. This, they—the Presidium—told the Comrade General this morning."

Golensky peered into his glass. Feeling his thin blood dance with repressed excitement, he went straight to the point. "Comrade Colonel, do they want him killed?"

Yatselev, the tricky part having now arrived, wiped a damp palm over his lips. "The Presidium has, comrade, in the presence of the Comrade General, indicated that, with Fitch gone, our . . ." he hesitated, ". . . our . . . policies . . . would, shall we say, progress with greater, one could say, facility."

"But, do they want him *killed?*"

"The implication is clear."

"Implication!" There it was, Golensky thought. The same old story. An objective to be accomplished, but everyone, even the great Presidium, ducking responsibility. Nevertheless, an exciting prospect. Some real game, regardless of who took responsibility. So, he added, "I understand, Yakov Petrovitch. And, I am ready."

Yatselev continued, as if there had been no interruption. "The Presidium has, as I said, given the Comrade General an indication of a course of action, and I have here, in my hand"—he picked up the black folder—"a summary of the file on George Wilson Fitch, sent to us by the Comrade General. Our duty is quite apparent, is it not?"

Golensky, resigning himself to the inevitable "scattering" of responsibility, responded, "Very well. It will be tricky, but it should not be *too* difficult. Let's see, he's going to the Far East next week, is he not? Well, then, perhaps a bomb . . ."

"*No!*"

"Well, if . . ."

"No!" Yatselev repeated. "It must be done with finesse. As if . . . it never happened."

"As if it never happened!" Golensky barked. "How can you kill the American Secretary of State as if it never happened? If we kill him, he will be dead, won't he?"

Softly, Yatselev answered, "Yes."

"Well, then . . ."

Yatselev smiled his puffy smile. "Ah, old friend, you see, that is why I am the Colonel and you are the Major."

Golensky grunted.

Yatselev pressed another button. This time an attractive, surprisingly slim, and well-groomed young woman entered the neuter-green room.

Yatselev, with a slight, almost erotic smile, said, "Ah, Mitya. Yes. The file, please, on the business of the saltshaker."

Golensky questioned, "The saltshaker business? But, surely, that is, you are saying . . . radioactive . . . ?"

"Yes," Yatselev responded crisply, "the saltshaker business. It will, I believe, be something like that, only not so quick . . . more subtle . . ."

Golensky, on the scent, "Yes, yes, Comrade Colonel! Should I summon an expert—Vorashkin, perhaps?"

"Not yet, not yet."

The girl returned, carrying a thick, yellow file.

Golensky perspired.

Yatselev ran his tongue over his lips with an almost obscene noise, and rapidly thumbed the file.

Golensky yelped, "*I* know what is in that file. It is only a question of how we place the stuff, and how much, where, and how . . ."

Yatselev raised his hand, authority in the gesture. Golensky had had sufficient time to digest the initial information, he thought. Closing the file, he said, "Yes, yes Fyodor Pavlovitch, old friend, comrade, you are, as always, correct. Call in Vorashkin."

While they waited for Semyon Vorashkin, the Kremlin's senior adviser on matters such as the effects of radioactive material on the human body, Yatselev raised his glass to himself. With a lip-smacking *"vashe zdarovie,"* he murmured, "You know, Fyodor Pavlovitch, our Mr. Fitch is quite famous for his love of caviar; we could, perhaps . . . that is, if it is to happen without happening . . ."

Golensky made a mind-leap. "Yes! But, if it is caviar, it must be *only* for the target . . . if it is to appear to have not happened at all."

III

The press, even in Moscow, bannered the story of the rapid recovery from an operation for acute cancer of the American Secretary of State, George Wilson Fitch.

Colonel Yakov Petrovitch Yatselev sat alone in Room 202, and stared, in disbelief, at the headlines. Indecent! *"Recovered,* indeed!" His fist slammed down on one of the numerous concealed buttons. Then, with an unusual show of emotion, he hurled the papers at the door.

Kicking aside the pages of *Izvestia,* Major Golensky strode through the door, smiling.

"Fyodor Pavlovitch!" Yatselev thundered, "You have *failed!"*

Disbelief registered on Golensky's calculating face. He protestsed, "But, Comrade Colonel, I do not understand."

"You don't understand!" Yatselev bellowed. "Don't you read the reports? Don't you read *Izvestia?"*

"But, Comrade Colonel—Yakov Petrovitch—it happened, shall we say, before the final assault."

"That he recovered?" Yatselev screamed.

"No, Comrade Colonel," Golensky responded,

looking hurt and adding, "That he got sick, which, of course, was, I think, in line with instructions, and he did *seem* done for . . ."

"You thought that he was done for?" Yatselev's scream was like a wire string ready to snap. "What are you saying? Are you trying, in some devious way, to cover your error . . . this is *not* a chess game . . . what are you saying?"

Golensky, his face giving off its finest air of underfed confusion, said, "But, we had a plan, you know, the caviar, and, well," with a smile, "we are, after all, Yakov Petrovitch, a nation of chess players, and, as you know, good chess players do not announce their moves, their methods—but, then, of course, he got sick first, shall we say, and we could not carry out the assault. Extraordinary coincidence, wouldn't you say, Yakov Petrovitch?"

Yatselev's usually florid face now matched the neuter-green walls, "You mean, you mean—no! This is *not* a chess game! That is, you mean . . . chess? . . . no . . . you mean, you are saying, that, that, that . . . this . . . cancer occurred from, from, that is . . ." as if afraid to say it, "from, from . . . *natural* causes?"

"But of course, Comrade Colonel. Otherwise, he would be dead, would he not?"

"I just do not understand. The Presidium thinks, the Comrade General thinks . . . I thought, Fyodor Pavlovitch, *I* thought that, that . . . but, I don't understand, and," slamming his hand to the desk with a fleshy thud, "this is impossible!"

Golensky, a bright, cheerful smile lighting his face, said, "But, Comrade Colonel, Fitch is leaving the hospital next week, and, then, as has been said . . . as if it never happened."

Yatselev gave Golensky a hard, formal stare.
"Comrade Major, are you telling me everything?"
"But of course, Comrade Colonel, but of course."

IV

Two years later, *Izvestia* again featured George Wilson Fitch, this time to announce his burial in that great memorial park for capitalist heroes, Arlington National Cemetery. Fitch, according to *Izvestia*, failed in a valiant fight against cancer, a fight so heroic that even citizens of the Soviet Union must "applaud his valor."

This copy of *Izvestia* was not, however, delivered to Room 202. For, like Arlington National Cemetery, Room 202 was silent, its new occupants not yet selected.

It was, indeed, as if it all never happened.

Is that the way it happened? Probably not. But, I remember being told that West German Chancellor Konrad Adenauer, upon learning of his friend Dulles' death, cried out in anguish, "It was the only way they could remove him."

And I have been haunted by the words of James Jesus Angleton, the legendary CIA counterintelligence chief, who, when asked, after his resignation, about the assassination of John F. Kennedy, was quoted as replying, "A mansion has many rooms . . . I'm not privy to who struck John."

Not that there is a connection. And, of course, it all, undoubtedly, just never happened.

Envoi

So, we close back near the beginning, on my first trip abroad with Dulles, when I was careening down a Paris hill from Montmartre in a cab with the Counsel for the Senate Armed Services Committee, my uncle, Fred B. Rhodes, Jr. His companion, a future Congressman, was throwing oranges out the window as the cab bounced up and down on cobblestones, and the driver was shrieking through the December cold that the oranges were a menace. Our future Congressman whistled at him and asked me what I would do if someone threw oranges at John Foster Dulles. I told him that someone *had* thrown a purple orange at Dulles, and he wanted to know how an orange could be purple, and not orange, but conversation stopped at that point because the driver was blowing his horn so that we would not be able to hear each other talk, and we were down the hill, speeding past the Madeleine and up to the Opera and the shops and the whores and the horse meat sellers, and then we were going right back up the hill to Montmartre. A few of the artists were still in the street and I was sure that they could not see anything except the pretty girls in turtleneck sweaters and leather coats and other things, and we chugged the climb to the Church of the Sacré Coeur, with a view of all Paris below.

Then we were skidding back down the hill, again, through fog-wisps, with houses falling down and slender streets and people-filled boulevards with all the bicycles and little cars and confusion, and we were going too fast. Horn blaring, we almost ran down four people. But we were going around the Petit Palais, past the Grand Palais, across the river to the Left Bank and, horn still blaring, back again to the Georges Cinq hotel, where Fred was staying. As the cab stopped, the horn stopped, and the future Congressman asked me what I would do if someone started throwing *orange* oranges at Dulles, and I said that I would throw them right back, and we were on the street and I was telling Fred the story that his brother Cooper had told of his coming into Paris as an American Colonel in the vanguard of the liberation and being one of the first American soldiers to sit down to dinner in the Georges Cinq with all its fine linen and silver and china and crystal gleaming in a velvetlike atmosphere of unknown luxuries just enjoyed by German officers, and the immaculate waiter entering and dramatically decorating each fine plate with a delicately sliced piece of Spam. Fred said that his father, my grandfather, had enjoyed that story, and would have enjoyed even more our standing in front of the Georges Cinq discussing it, and somebody raised the question of oranges again, stating that I had not truly addressed myself to the problem of *orange* oranges. That was true, but I had this wonderful feeling of being somewhere on the fringe of history, and I laughed at how ridiculous it all really was.